EDITOR:
Jack Harrison
jharrison@mortons.co.uk

PRODUCTION EDITOR:
Dan Sharp

DESIGNER:
Craig Lamb
design_lamb@btinternet.com

COVER DESIGN:
Holly Munro

REPROGRAPHICS:
Paul Fincham and Jonathan Schofield

PUBLISHERS:
Steve O'Hara, Tim Hartley

PUBLISHING DIRECTOR:
Dan Savage

COMMERCIAL DIRECTOR:
Nigel Hole

MARKETING MANAGER:
Charlotte Park
cpark@mortons.co.uk

DISTRIBUTION EXECUTIVE
John Sharratt
tradesales@mortons.co.uk
classicmagazines.co.uk/tradesales

PRINTED BY:
William Gibbons and Sons, Wolverhampton

ISBN:
978-1-909128-83-5

PUBLISHED BY:
Mortons Media Group Ltd,
Media Centre, Morton Way,
Horncastle, Lincolnshire LN9 6JR.
Tel: 01507 529529

COPYRIGHT:
Mortons Media Group Ltd, 2016
All rights reserved.

LEFT:

90 images from
the life of Queen
Elizabeth II.

The Queen at 90

Queen Elizabeth II has ruled Britain for more than six decades and this year celebrates her 90th birthday.

As the longest reigning monarch in British history, she has been a figurehead of consistency and tradition since the 1950s, and has worked tirelessly for the good of her people both at home and across the Commonwealth .

The hundreds of carefully chosen images in this volume trace the course of her reign – from her unwavering devotion to duty, to the moments of personal joy and sadness – and offer an opportunity to reflect on one of the century's greatest lives.

Preface

Queen Elizabeth. When I delved into the first archive collection on my list to explore in preparation for this publication I quickly came upon just short of 100,000 images captioned with those two words and it soon became abundantly clear that whittling them down to the 400-or-so I needed was going to be no simple task.

What also became immediately apparent as I began to research and discuss *The Queen at 90* is that most people have a very clearly defined idea of who the Queen is. It might be the stoic sovereign who has stuck resolutely to protocol and tradition on official occasions; perhaps it's the warm and personable leader who has found a way to connect with her subjects through countless public engagements; then there's the doting mother, grandmother and great-grandmother, leading her family through turbulent times; or maybe it's the skilled international stateswoman who has commanded respect and gained affection from some of the world's most powerful figures.

Another variable is age, both that of the person you ask and of the Queen. For many older readers it will be the Silver Jubilee Queen that automatically comes to mind; for those even older it might be the young princess who was thrust into a life of public service; and for comparative youngsters it is more likely to be the elder monarch presiding over an expanding royal family which has welcomed a number of new members between the birth of Peter Phillips in 1977 and the arrival Princess Charlotte in 2015.

Whichever image of the Queen seems most familiar to us, it's likely that our perception will have been shaped by the abundance of photographs and film that exists of her. Cameras have followed Her Majesty since 1926, capturing every moment of her life in public. And what a remarkable life it has been.

Think of any milestone moment in British – and often world – history in the last 90 years and the Queen has been there; many times at the forefront as a leader and many times as the subject of the story. Recall the iconic people of the last nine decades – be they politicians, heads of state, religious leaders, celebrities, other public figures – and there's every chance they will have crossed paths with the Queen.

The world is a very different place today to how it was in 1926 – advancements in technology, cultural shifts, political evolution and revolution; these are just some of the seismic changes to have occurred. Yet in a time where the only certainty is that nothing is certain, the Queen has remained a beacon of stability, recognised and respected by many across the globe.

If you're reading this then I suspect your view of the monarchy is a positive one, but whatever your opinion there can be little argument that this is a fascinating subject. A monarch able to switch between the different approaches required for different situations, a symbolic figurehead for several generations and an anchor throughout the last 90 years of world events – it's these three themes that I have tried to capture in presenting a pictorial history of Queen Elizabeth II to mark the occasion of her 90th birthday.

Choosing the more-than-400 images which form the heart of this bookazine has been a challenge, but most definitely not a chore. Learning more about the life of the Queen, our Queen, has been enlightening, and seeing history unfold through the camera lenses following Her Majesty to every corner of the globe has been a most thoroughly enjoyable experience. I sincerely hope I've conveyed that in these 134 pages, and that you enjoy the journey through time as much as I did.

Jack Harrison
EDITOR

Acknowledgements

There are a great many people and groups who deserve credit for helping with or contributing to this publication.
I am indebted to the talents of the design team – Craig Lamb (inside pages) and Holly Munro (cover) – for turning my words and chosen selection of images into this stylish finished product. My thanks must also go to production editor Dan Sharp for his expertise in guiding both myself and the publication through the process from initial idea to completed pages.
The Press Association image archive, which has provided the majority of photographs found within, is a fantastic resource for authors, editors and journalists and throughout my research I continued to be amazed at the depth and variety of royal content available. Complementing the PA selection is a range of images sourced from contributors who have shared their work using a Creative Commons Licence – creativecommons.org – a superb initiative which promotes the sharing of content throughout the world using online channels. The reprographics team – Paul Fincham and Jonathan Schofield – also deserve a mention for their sterling work in ensuring the print-readiness of all the images.
On a personal note, I also want to share my appreciation for the continued support and encouragement of my colleagues, friends, family and loved ones during the time spent working on The Queen at 90.

CONTENTS

Queen Elizabeth II
and The Queen
Mother at Sandown
Park races on
November 21,
1953.

At Buckingham Palace, Queen Elizabeth II sits and looks at some of the cards sent for the occasion of her 80th birthday, April 20, 2006. Fiona Hanson/PA Archive/PA Images

At the Cenotaph in Whitehall, Queen Elizabeth II places a wreath of red poppies as she leads the nation in tribute to the British military personnel who died in the First and Second World Wars, November 10, 1957.

Long to reign over us

For more than 60 years, large crowds have gathered across the country and across the world to mark the momentous occasions of Queen Elizabeth II's reign.

LEFT TO RIGHT:

The Coronation, London, June 2, 1953. Sport and General/ S&G Barratts/EMPICS Archive

The Silver Jubilee tour, Cardiff, June 24, 1977. Ron Bell/PA Archive/ PA Images

The Golden Jubilee, London, June 4, 2002. Chris Ison/PA Archive/ PA Images

The Diamond Jubilee, London, June 5, 2012. Anwar Hussein/ EMPICS Entertainment

Her Majesty becomes the longest-reigning monarch, Tweedbank, September 9, 2015 Scott Heppell/AP/ Press Association Images

On September 9, 2015, Queen Elizabeth II and the Duke of Edinburgh travelled by steam train from Edinburgh to Tweedbank to formally open the new £294 million Scottish Borders Railway. It was the type of official engagement with which Her Majesty has become synonymous, but this was no ordinary event.

That day, at 5.30pm, Queen Elizabeth II became Great Britain's longest-reigning monarch – surpassing the 63 years and seven months of her great-great-grandmother Queen Victoria.

In a speech at the opening of the railway she said: "Inevitably a long life can pass by many milestones – my own is no exception – but I thank you all and the many others at home and overseas for your touching messages of great kindness." This understated approach reflected Queen Elizabeth II's wishes that the day not be one of great fuss, but there were a series of tributes paid across the country – including in the House of Commons – and HMS Belfast sounded a four-gun salute.

When Her Majesty's reign began in the early hours of February 6, 1952, there had been five British sovereigns in the first five decades of the 20th century – including the 'Year of Three Kings' in 1936 when King George V, King Edward VIII and King George VI all reigned. A nation that had experienced two world wars and a global financial crash needed a beacon of stability, and that had arrived in the form of Queen Elizabeth II.

The coronation on June 2, 1953, provided a reason to look to the future and celebrate the notion of better times, and some three million subjects did exactly that as they lined the streets of London hoping to get a view of Her Majesty's procession.

The national and international celebrations that have marked her milestone moments since then have been of vital importance in providing moments of reflection and in serving to reinvigorate the royal institution. In 1977 the country would celebrate Queen Elizabeth II's 25 years on the throne during the Silver Jubilee which was held to coincide with the Queen's Official Birthday in June.

While the coronation was a large-scale event, the fact that it was taking place less than eight years after the end of the Second World War meant there were constraints – something which didn't apply to 1977.

On June 6, Queen Elizabeth II lit a bonfire beacon at Windsor Castle which was followed by a chain of further beacons being lit across the country. The following day, huge crowds lined the route of a procession to St Paul's Cathedral where the royal family attended a service of thanksgiving which was attended by many world leaders and senior figures including US President Jimmy Carter.

From June 1-4, 2002, the Golden Jubilee Weekend opened with the Prom at the Palace classical music event which took place in the gardens of Buckingham Palace and became the largest event held on royal property.

Evoking memories of the Silver Jubilee, Queen Elizabeth II lit a beacon at the Victoria Memorial which completed the lighting of 2006 beacons throughout the world, before she and the Duke of Edinburgh arrived by golden stagecoach at a thanksgiving service at St Paul's Cathedral on June 4. Later that day, the royal family assembled on the Buckingham Palace balcony to watch a flypast of all 27 different active Royal Air Force aircraft types, Concorde and the Red Arrows.

Only once before had a monarch, Queen Victoria in 1897, been able to mark 60 years on the throne and so by 2012 and Queen Elizabeth II's Diamond Jubilee, celebrations had extended from a weekend to a series of events that took place throughout the whole year. The June weekend of Her Majesty's official birthday remained central however, and included both June 4 and 5 being made Bank Holidays to create a four-day Diamond Jubilee weekend. A wide variety of commemorative efforts were made, but many of the central elements of previous jubilees were retained – giving proceedings the sense of continuity and tradition that has become Queen Elizabeth II's trademark.

On April 21, 2016, the Queen celebrates her 90th birthday. As with the jubilee celebrations throughout her reign, events will take place across the country and throughout the Commonwealth to mark the occasion with a pageant planned for May 12-15 at Windsor Castle being the first major date in the calendar.

Queen Elizabeth II smiles on the day she became Great Britain's longest-reigning monarch – September 9, 2015. Andrew Milligan/PA Wire/Press Association Images

The Coronation, 1953

Following the coronation ceremony at Westminster Abbey, Queen Elizabeth II prepares to enter the State Coach and make her return to Buckingham Palace.

The Queen Mother waves to crowds following the coronation of her daughter.

Wearing the Imperial Crown, Queen Elizabeth II smiles and waves to the crowd from Buckingham Palace.

A huge crowd gathers on The Mall, waiting to see Queen Elizabeth II step on to the Buckingham Palace balcony.

The royal family stand on the balcony of Buckingham Palace to view the Royal Air Force's coronation flypast.

Queen Elizabeth II stands with the Duke of Edinburgh, The Queen Mother and Princess Margaret at Buckingham Palace to mark her coronation.

The Silver Jubilee, 1977

Queen Elizabeth II lights the Jubilee bonfire at Snow Hill, Windsor Great Park, to mark the start of the 1977 celebrations. Ron Bell/PA Archive/PA Images

Excited onlookers cheer Queen Elizabeth II in Portsmouth during the Silver Jubilee tour.

In the sitting room of Windsor Castle, Queen Elizabeth II looks at photographs taken during the Silver Jubilee tour of the South Pacific and Australasia.

Queen Elizabeth II and the Duke of Edinburgh kneel during the Silver Jubilee Thanksgiving Service in St Paul's Cathedral.

The royal family watches the Silver Jubilee procession from the Buckingham Palace balcony.

After landing at Lambeth Pier following her Silver Jubilee river progress from Greenwich, Queen Elizabeth II meets men of the London Fire Brigade at their headquarters. Ron Bell/PA Archive/PA Images

The Golden Jubilee, 2002

The royal family stand with the congregation at the Golden Jubilee Thanksgiving Service in St Paul's Cathedral. Andrew Parsons/PA Archive/PA Images

The golden State Coach was built in 1762 for King George III and before the Golden Jubilee had only been used twice by Her Majesty – the coronation and the Silver Jubilee. Queen Elizabeth II and the Duke of Edinburgh used the carriage to travel to St Paul's Cathedral for a thanksgiving service. Stefan Rousseau/PA Archive/PA Images

A unique and historic parade of ceremonial royal body guards and Chelsea Pensioners greet Queen Elizabeth II at Buckingham Palace. The event was the first of its kind, arranged in honour of the Golden Jubilee. Kirsty Wigglesworth/ PA Archive/PA Images

During a Golden Jubilee visit to All Saints Church in Kingston-upon-Thames, Queen Elizabeth II accepts floral bouquets from local schoolgirls. Fiona Hanson/PA Archive/PA Images

Queen Elizabeth II is joined on the Buckingham Palace balcony by performers from the Prom at the Palace – the first public concert ever staged in the grounds of the royal residence. Peter Jordan/PA Archive/PA Images

Jockeys riding in the Champagne Victor Queen's Golden Jubilee handicap stakes at Beverley meet Her Majesty ahead of the race. Gareth Copley/PA Archive/PA Images

The Diamond Jubilee, 2012

Queen Elizabeth II waves to crowds from the Buckingham Palace balcony, flanked by other members of the royal family. David Jones/PA Archive/PA Images

As with previous jubilee celebrations, the royal family attend a thanksgiving service at St Paul's Cathedral. Suzanne Plunkett/PA Archive/PA Images

On board the *Spirit of Chartwell*, Queen Elizabeth II, the Duchess of Cornwall and the Duchess of Cambridge enjoy the Diamond Jubilee Pageant as they travel along the River Thames. David Crump/Daily Mail/PA Archive/PA Images

Clearly enjoying the occasion, Queen Elizabeth II watches the action at Epsom in Surrey on Derby Day. Steve Parsons/PA Archive/PA Images

Backstage at the Buckingham Palace Diamond Jubilee concert, Queen Elizabeth II meets Sir Elton John, Sir Cliff Richard, Dame Shirley Bassey, Sir Tom Jones and Sir Paul McCartney. Dave Thompson/PA Archive/PA Images

The Red Arrows fly above Buckingham Palace to conclude the four-day Diamond Jubilee celebrations – the royal family looking on from the balcony. Lefteris Pitarakis/AP/Press Association Images

A princess is born

Queen Elizabeth II was born at 2.40am on Wednesday, April 21, 1926. To little fuss or fanfare, she arrived into the world as a princess at 17 Bruton Street, Mayfair, London, the first child of the Duke and Duchess of York – later King George VI and Queen Elizabeth, The Queen Mother – who had been married a little less than three years earlier on April 26, 1923, at a Westminster Abbey ceremony. The venue for her birth was the private home of the Earl and Countess of Strathmore, the parents of the Duchess of York and the princess's grandparents.

A month later, she was christened Elizabeth Alexandra Mary in the private chapel at Buckingham Palace. She was named after her mother, Elizabeth Angela Marguerite Bowes-Lyon, with her middle names being taken from her great-grandmother – Alexandra of Denmark the Queen Consort of King Edward VII – and her grandmother – Mary of Teck the Queen Consort of King George V.

There was public interest in the new princess, but with radio in its infancy and in a time before television there was a vast contrast between this 1920s event and the frenzied national attention given to royal births in the later part of the 20th century and new millennium.

Although there was no immediate way to cover the news, the fact was that Princess Elizabeth was now third in line to the throne behind her father and the king's oldest son Edward, the Prince of Wales. Edward was still a young man at the age of 31 and there was no reason to doubt that he would go on to have children of his own. If he did then they would supersede Princess Elizabeth in the line of succession, so while there's no doubt that she was always going to be a prominent member of the royal family, it seemed unlikely that the princess would ever become queen.

This allowed 'Lilibet' – as she was known to her family for the way she first attempted to pronounce her own name – to grow up out of the spotlight in the relatively quiet and uneventful surroundings of 145 Piccadilly, the London home taken by her parents after her birth, and then at White Lodge in Richmond Park. She would also spend a lot of time at the country homes of both sets of grandparents as the Duke and Duchess of York undertook their royal engagements which at the time meant lengthy voyages by ship to all corners of the British Empire.

The events which would unfold in the years after the death of King George V in 1936 would change the course of British and world history, and take Princess Elizabeth on a path that surely even she could have never foreseen. Before that time, in her formative years, she lived a life largely out of the glare of public and press attention and only a handful of images of the future monarch exist.

The royal wave has been a familiar image throughout her reign, but these were among the first to be given by a two-year-old Princess Elizabeth travelling through London by carriage in May 1928.

Proud new parents the Duke and Duchess of York present their eight-day-old daughter Princess Elizabeth in what is one of the very first pictures of the future Queen, April 29, 1926.

Princess Elizabeth's family tree

Lineage and ancestry

Princess Elizabeth, later Queen Elizabeth II
BORN: April 21, 1926

Princess Elizabeth was born as the paternal or male-line great-granddaughter of King Edward VII who had succeeded to the throne following the death of his mother, Queen Victoria. As great-great-granddaughter of Queen Victoria, Queen Elizabeth has links to most reigning and non-reigning European royal houses and is also directly descended from the House of Stuart; Mary, Queen of Scots; Robert the Bruce and earlier Scottish royal houses; the House of Tudor and earlier English and Irish royal houses going back as far as the seventh century House of Wessex.

King Edward VII's wife and the princess's great-grandmother Queen Alexandra of Denmark gives her family ties to the Danish House of Schleswig-Holstein-Sonderburg-Glücksburg, itself a line of the North German House of Oldenburg which included Princess Elizabeth's future husband Prince Philip of Greece and Denmark.

Through Queen Victoria's consort Prince Albert – earlier Albert of Saxe-Coburg and Gotha, Princess Elizabeth was born into a paternal or male-line ancestry that can be traced back to Theodoric I, Count of Wettin. Although little is known about Theodoric's life more than 1000 years ago, he is believed to be the oldest traceable member of the House of Wettin which has produced many of the dukes, electors and kings of Saxony.

Princess Elizabeth, three years old, from the cover of *Time* magazine, 1929.

Parents and grandparents

King George V

BORN: June 3, 1865
DIED: January 20, 1936
KING: May 6, 1910-January 20, 1936

RELATIONSHIP TO PRINCESS ELIZABETH: **Paternal grandfather**

Claude George Bowes-Lyon, Earl of Strathmore and Kinghorne

BORN: March 14, 1855
DIED: November 7, 1944

RELATIONSHIP TO PRINCESS ELIZABETH: **Maternal grandfather**

Mary of Teck, Queen Consort Queen Mary

BORN: May 26, 1867
DIED: March 24, 1953

RELATIONSHIP TO PRINCESS ELIZABETH: **Paternal grandmother**

Cecilia Nina Bowes-Lyon, Countess of Strathmore and Kinghorne

BORN: September 11, 1862
DIED: June 23, 1938

RELATIONSHIP TO PRINCESS ELIZABETH: **Maternal grandmother**

The Duke of York, later King George VI

BORN: December 14, 1895
DIED: February 6, 1952
KING: December 11, 1936-February 6, 1952

RELATIONSHIP TO PRINCESS ELIZABETH: **Father**

Elizabeth Bowes-Lyon, Duchess of York, later The Queen Mother

BORN: August 4, 1900
DIED: March 30, 2002

RELATIONSHIP TO PRINCESS ELIZABETH: **Mother**

Princess Elizabeth was christened Elizabeth Alexandra Mary by the Anglican Archbishop of York, Cosmo Gordon Lang, in Buckingham Palace's private chapel on May 29, 1926. The christening party is pictured.

Front row, left to right:
Lady Elphinstone, elder sister of the Duchess of York and godparent to Princess Elizabeth
Mary of Teck, Queen consort to King George V
The Duchess of York holding the baby Princess Elizabeth
The Countess of Strathmore, mother of the Duchess of York and godparent to Princess Elizabeth
Princess Mary, daughter of King George V and Queen Consort Queen Mary

Back row, left to right:
Prince Arthur, son of Queen Victoria and Prince Albert
King George V
The Duke of York standing behind his wife and daughter
The Earl of Strathmore, father of the Duchess of York

The Duke and Duchess of York (both left) hold one-year-old Princess Elizabeth on the balcony of Buckingham Palace on June 27, 1927. Queen Consort Queen Mary shades the youngster with an umbrella with King George V standing behind his granddaughter.

A Highland Regiment drummer plays on while Princess Elizabeth listens during a visit to Scotland, January 1929.

Princess Elizabeth playing in her garden at 145 Piccadilly, the house taken by her parents the Duke and Duchess of York shortly after her birth, June 1928.

Princess Elizabeth (left) being taken for a ride around the grounds of Windsor Castle with her cousin Gerald Lascelles, the son of Princess Mary, 1927.

Princess Elizabeth enjoying a carriage ride with her nanny near Battersea Park, March 1929.

Princess Elizabeth stays close to her mother's side as they walk through London's Lowndes Square in June 1929. The upmarket area of Belgravia was home to the Earl of Strathmore, grandfather to Princess Elizabeth. Today the neighbourhood is home to some of Britain's wealthiest residents, including Russian oligarch Roman Abramovich.

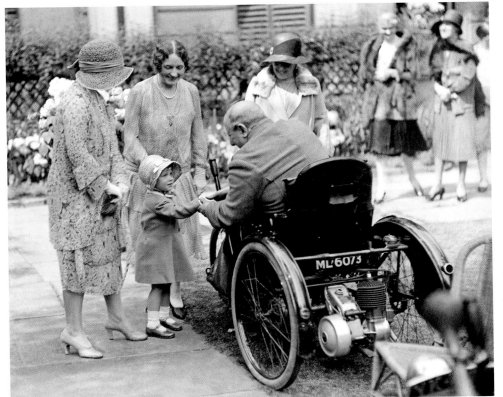

An elderly ex-serviceman is embraced by Princess Elizabeth at an exhibition of disabled soldiers' embroideries in London, June 13, 1929.

The 1930s

In the space of a year, Princess Elizabeth had gone from a comparatively quiet royal upbringing to being first in line to the throne with only a son born to her parents able to supersede her. It was not a life she had prepared for in her early years, but she seemed to take it all in her stride. She's pictured alongside her mother – Queen Consort Queen Elizabeth – in full regal attire on the balcony of Buckingham Palace following the coronation of her father King George VI, May 12, 1937.

For Princess Elizabeth the 1930s started how the previous decade had finished; the privilege of a royal lifestyle without the intense pressure of being directly in line to the throne and without having to contend with the sort of press spotlight which would shine brightly on her future reign as Queen.

On August 21, 1930, with even less coverage than her own birth, Princess Elizabeth gained a sister as Princess Margaret Rose came into the world at Scotland's Glamis Castle, the ancestral home of her mother the Duchess of York. Like her older sibling, Princess Margaret was baptised in the private chapel of Buckingham Palace by Cosmo Lang, now the Archbishop of Canterbury.

The Duke, Duchess and their two children were seen by the public as the perfect family; happily married mother and father and two young princesses who had it all. Despite the parents having to fulfil royal duties, the four were close and the two sisters especially formed a bond as youngsters as they played together and were privately educated as a pair.

Throughout her childhood Princess Elizabeth was close with her grandfather King George V – he was the one who had given her the nickname 'Lilibet' – and she was known to affectionately refer to him as Grandpa England. The perfect family which her father had built also impressed the King, something which was in stark contrast to the controversial playboy lifestyle of his eldest son and heir Edward, Prince of Wales.

At the start of 1936, the King's health began to deteriorate and on January 20 it was announced that he had passed away peacefully in his sleep and his eldest son Edward would ascend to the throne as King Edward VIII. The new monarch caused unease among British institutions and although his approach in many ways brought about a modernised monarchy, when it became clear he intended to marry American divorcee Wallis Simpson his future as King was called into question by church and state alike.

By December 1936, King Edward VIII faced three choices: giving up the woman he loved, marrying her against government wishes and causing a constitutional crisis or abdicating the throne; he opted for the latter and King George VI was crowned in his place.

Princess Elizabeth, just 12 years old, was now next in line and unless her parents were to have a son before she ascended it was highly likely she would become Queen of the United Kingdom and its territories. Along with her private education, she began to prepare for the role that now awaited her.

As heiress-apparent, Princess Elizabeth was much more in the public eye than had previously been the case as interest grew in the new occupants of Buckingham Palace. Public duties were also introduced to the princess's schedule, although these generally involved accompanying her mother to various functions and events.

On September 3, 1939, a turbulent decade was concluded with the outbreak of the Second World War and as many of London's children were evacuated from the city, Princesses Elizabeth and Margaret were taken to Scotland's Balmoral Castle until Christmas when they moved into Sandringham House in Norfolk. The Government suggested that the sisters be taken to Canada, but Queen Consort Queen Elizabeth responded to this suggestion by saying: "The children won't go without me. I won't leave the King. And the King will never leave."

The peoples of the United Kingdom and the Empire quickly warmed to their new royal family with the happily married parents and two young children living a clean-cut idyllic family life to which a nation could aspire. King George VI and Queen Consort Queen Elizabeth stand proudly with Princesses Elizabeth and Margaret on the day of His Majesty's coronation, May 12, 1937.

Princess Elizabeth would spend much of her childhood in the beautiful surroundings of Windsor Castle. She is pictured in the distance riding a horse with the building in the background – one of the earliest images of her enjoying what would become a cherished pastime, 1930.

A two-year-old Princess Margaret sits next to her older sister Princess Elizabeth, aged seven, 1933.

Childhood fun for Princess Elizabeth as she rides a tricycle through the park, 1933.

A young princess at play... the Duke of York took this picture of his daughter among Madonna lilies. The photo was released on May 30, 1930, as part of a royal photography exhibition on behalf of King Edward's Hospital Fund for London and voluntary hospitals. Duke of York/AP/Press Association Images

Princess Elizabeth (centre) enjoys the company of friends at the sixth birthday celebrations of James Carnegie, later 3rd Duke of Fife, at Elsick House in Kincardineshire, now Aberdeenshire, on September 23, 1935. The full line-up, from left to right: Zoe d'Erlanger, Princess Margaret, James Carnegie, Princess Elizabeth, Mary Anna Stunt and Master Wolrige-Gordon.

Accompanied by her riding master, Princess Elizabeth celebrates her 10th birthday on her new white pony in Windsor Great Park on April 21, 1936.

A love of dogs – particularly Corgis – would become one of her most famous traits and Princess Elizabeth is pictured walking her pet in London's Hyde Park, February 26, 1936.

Princess Elizabeth holds a Pembrokeshire Corgi while Princess Margaret feeds the pet a biscuit as the two sisters enjoy a relaxing summer afternoon, July 5, 1936.

Even from an early age, Princess Elizabeth seemed comfortable with her position, status and royal duties. She is pictured waving confidently from the Buckingham Palace balcony following a jubilee thanksgiving service on May 6, 1935. Her grandfather King George V and grandmother Queen Consort Queen Mary stand alongside, with a four-year-old Princess Margaret just tall enough to peer over the ledge.

Princesses Elizabeth and Margaret join their parents for the Royal Tournament at London's Olympia, May 1, 1936.

Enjoying the fun at London Zoo, Princess Elizabeth and her companion Shaun Plunket take the penguins for a walk on June 30, 1938. The young boy is the son of Lord and Lady Plunket, long-time family friends of the royal household.

Once her father had become King and was required to fulfil royal duties abroad, Princess Elizabeth was often the senior member of the royal household during public appearances. In this picture, she enjoys her first ride on an elephant at London Zoo with her sister Princess Margaret with King George VI and Queen Consort Queen Elizabeth on a voyage to the USA, May 10, 1939.

Before moving to Buckingham Palace when their father became King George VI, number 145 Piccadilly was home to Princesses Elizabeth and Margaret.

The Abdication Crisis

At Fort Belvedere in Windsor Great Park on December 10, 1936, King Edward VIII signed his written abdication notices and gave up the throne of the United Kingdom. Less than a year earlier on January 20 he had succeeded his father, George V, and had almost immediately courted controversy as he proposed marriage to American socialite Wallis Simpson.

Mrs Simpson was divorced from her first husband and in the process of divorcing her second; political and religious leaders were outraged and vehemently opposed the notion that a king could marry a divorcee. Such an act was not allowed by the Church of England, of which the English monarch is the titular head. Mrs Simpson was also viewed as politically unstable and an unsuitable consort.

Despite these protests, King Edward VIII reaffirmed his love for Mrs Simpson and stated his intention to marry her with or without the support and blessing of government and church. The widespread unwillingness to allow this led to His Majesty relinquishing the crown and he became the only British monarch to have voluntarily stepped aside since the Anglo-Saxon period.

King Edward VIII was succeeded by his brother, the Duke of York, who took the name King George VI. Princess Elizabeth was now heir to the throne of the United Kingdom; the quiet and peaceful upbringing she'd enjoyed, largely out of the limelight, had become an adolescence that would be spent under the intense glare of the public spotlight.

Edward, given the title Duke of Windsor, married Mrs Simpson on June 3, 1937, in France and the couple remained together until his death on May 28, 1972.

Edward, Prince of Wales, is joined by his niece Princess Elizabeth at the Highland Games and Gathering at Braemar on October 26, 1932.

The Duke and Duchess of Windsor – formerly King Edward VIII and Wallis Simpson – pose on the castle steps after their wedding at Chateau de Cande near Tours, France, June 3, 1937.

King Edward VIII makes his first broadcast to the nation on March 1, 1936. A little over seven months later he would once again speak to his subjects, but this time to notify them of his abdication.

King George VI and Queen Consort Queen Elizabeth receive 1000 Girl Guides from all parts of the UK at Windsor Castle on June 19, 1938. Princesses Elizabeth and Margaret appear in uniform, both of them as members of the 1st Buckingham Palace Company, which was formed on June 9, 1937, so that Elizabeth could become a Girl Guide. The 20-strong company comprised children from the royal household and palace employees. Meetings took place at the royal residence, before moving to Windsor Castle during the Second World War. A Brownie Pack was also created for Margaret which had 14 members. The company was re-formed in 1959 for Queen Elizabeth II's daughter Princess Anne and remained active until 1963.

Princess Elizabeth – aged 13 – and her eight-year-old sister just behind take their first ride on a tube train on May 15, 1939. The sisters rode in a normal coach, mingling with other passengers, as they travelled from St James's Park to Tottenham Court Road. Eddie Worth/AP/Press Association Images

Princesses Elizabeth and Margaret join thousands of spectators at Rushmoor Arena for the daylight rehearsal of the Aldershot Tattoo on June 7, 1938. Queen Consort Queen Elizabeth was due to attend but pulled out because of a cold, leaving her 12-year-old daughter as the senior member in the royal box. She is pictured receiving a programme from top military officer Sir John Dill.

Declaration of war

On September 3, 1939, Britain declared war on Germany in response to the invasion of Poland. A little more than two decades since the end of 'the Great War', the country once again found itself facing the upheaval and threats brought about by global conflict.

Still coming to terms with the notion of being the direct heir to the throne, Princess Elizabeth now had to contend with the knowledge that her father was king of a country embroiled in a bitter and dangerous world war. It was an uncertain time for the nation.

A short time after the official declaration by Prime Minister Neville Chamberlain, King George VI addressed his subjects with a radio broadcast – his first to the nation. The historic moment has been popularised in the 2010 film The King's Speech starring Colin Firth in the lead role. Although short in words, King George's delivery meant it lasted longer than five minutes:

"In this grave hour, perhaps the most fateful in our history, I send to every household of my peoples, both at home and overseas, this message, spoken with the same depth of feeling for each one of you as if I were able to cross your threshold and speak to you myself. For the second time in the lives of most of us we are at war. Over and over again we have tried to find a peaceful way out of the differences between ourselves and those who are now our enemies. But it has been in vain.

We have been forced into a conflict. For we are called, with our allies, to meet the challenge of a principle which, if it were to prevail, would be fatal to any civilized order in the world. It is the principle which permits a state, in the selfish pursuit of power, to disregard its treaties and its solemn pledges; which sanctions the use of force, or threat of force, against the sovereignty and independence of other states.

Such a principle, stripped of all disguise, is surely the mere primitive doctrine that 'might is right'; and if this principle were established throughout the world, the freedom of our own country and of the whole of the British Commonwealth of Nations would be in danger. But far more than this – the peoples of the world would be kept in the bondage of fear, and all hopes of settled peace and of the security of justice and liberty among nations would be ended.

This is the ultimate issue which confronts us. For the sake of all that we ourselves hold dear, and of the world order and peace, it is unthinkable that we should refuse to meet the challenge. It is to this high purpose that I now call my people at home and my peoples across the seas, who will make our cause their own.

I ask them to stand calm and firm and united in this time of trial. The task will be hard. There may be dark days ahead, and war can no longer be confined to the battlefield. But we can only do the right as we see the right, and reverently commit our cause to God. If one and all we keep resolutely faithful to it, ready for whatever service or sacrifice it may demand, then, with God's help, we shall prevail. May He bless and keep us all."

King George VI
Radio address
September 3, 1939

King George VI delivers his famous radio address which became the subject of Oscar-winning film The King's Speech.

The 1940s

As the 1940s dawned, the United Kingdom and Empire faced the terrors of the Second World War as Nazi Germany sought global domination. Princesses Elizabeth and Margaret were now residing at Windsor Castle where they would remain for the majority of the war.

The royal sisters played a vital role during those years, leading by example to support the efforts being made at home as thousands of British men were leaving to fight abroad. Within the grounds of Windsor the two had grown allotments, would use ponies and carts to travel and continued to participate in the Girl Guides and Brownies, learning the vital skills that were expected of young women of the time.

With the pressures of war mounting, the country needed a strong figurehead and Princess Elizabeth – now in her teens and with the growing responsibility of being the firstborn child of the King – helped to fulfil this role. In 1940 she made her first radio broadcast, addressing fellow children who had been evacuated from Britain's major cities. In 1943, she undertook her first solo public appearance, visiting the Grenadier Guards.

As she approached her 18th birthday in 1944, a change in the law meant the age at which a royal appointment could be taken up was lowered, having previously been 21. Princess Elizabeth was made a Counsellor of State so that in the event of her father being incapacitated or absent from the country she was permitted to carry out several of his duties. It was a decision that was neither ceremonial nor symbolic; the country was still embroiled in battle and the threat of harm coming to the King was very real.

In February 1945, Princess Elizabeth formally joined the war effort, becoming part of the women's Auxiliary Territorial Service and training as a driver and mechanic. While the conflict was in its closing stages at this time, it was a move which generated much public support and goodwill for the future Queen.

As Europe revelled in the euphoria of VE Day on May 8, 1945, Princesses Elizabeth and Margaret famously went incognito to join Londoners in their celebrations – an episode which has gone down in folklore and has been dramatised in film. At the start of the Second World War, Princess Elizabeth was a 13-year-old girl but by the time it ended and as the United Kingdom looked to settle into life after wartime she had become a young woman.

Now a senior member of the royal family, Princess Elizabeth accompanied her parents on their royal tour to Africa in 1947. While on the trip she celebrated her 21st birthday and to mark the occasion she made a special broadcast to the Commonwealth in which she said: "I declare before you all that my whole life, whether it be long or short, shall be devoted to your service and the service of our great imperial family to which we all belong."

It was also at this time that she turned attention to her personal life and started a family of her own.

Princesses Elizabeth and Margaret were crucial in setting an example to the nation with their home-front efforts during the Second World War. The sisters are pictured picking dwarf beans from their own allotments at Windsor Castle during the summer of 1943.

The two sisters also inspect tomatoes they have grown in their own garden.

During ceremonies at the No 1 MT Training Centre at Camberly, Surrey – a training camp for the Auxiliary Territorial Service (ATS) of which she was a part – Princess Elizabeth is presented with a clock by associates on August 3, 1945. Often pronounced as the acronym, the ATS was a women's branch of the British Army during the Second World War. At the point of its formation in 1938 it was a voluntary organisation, but the National Service Act of December 1941 meant unmarried women aged 20-30 could be called up to join the auxiliary military services. Women were disqualified from serving in battle, but due to the number of men who were away from home or who had died in service, ATS members took over many support tasks such as radar and anti-aircraft operations. Princess Elizabeth joined the ATS in February 1945 as an honorary second subaltern – equivalent to a second lieutenant – and trained as a driver and mechanic. She was promoted to honorary junior commander five months later.

Princesses Elizabeth and Margaret practice their bandaging skills as part of their Girl Guide duties in 1943. The elder sister is wearing the badge of the swallow patrol and two white stripes, indicating that she is a patrol leader.

The threat faced by the royal family during the Second World War was a very real one, and King George VI and Queen Consort Queen Elizabeth are pictured amid bomb damage at Buckingham Palace on September 10, 1940. The Luftwaffe attempted to target the royal residence, with Nazi Germany believing that its destruction would demoralise the nation. It had the opposite effect however, the King's wife famously saying: "I'm glad we have been bombed. Now I can look the East End in the face."

Princess Margaret looks on as Princess Elizabeth holds a carrier pigeon which she will release with a message to Lady Baden-Powell on February 22, 1943. It was one of many liberated on Thinking Day, which marks the birthday of Lord Baden-Powell, the founder of the Scout movement.

First public broadcast

On October 13, 1940, a 14-year-old Princess Elizabeth made her first public broadcast as part of BBC Children's Hour. She spoke directly to the young people of the United Kingdom who had been evacuated and were living away from their homes during the Second World War, and was joined at the end of the address by her sister Princess Margaret:

"In wishing you all good evening, I feel that I am speaking to friends and companions who have shared with my sister and myself many a happy Children's Hour. Thousands of you in this country have had to leave your homes and be separated from your fathers and mothers. My sister Margaret Rose and I feel so much for you as we know from experience what it means to be away from those we love most of all.

To you, living in new surroundings, we send a message of true sympathy and at the same time we would like to thank the kind people who have welcomed you to their homes in the country. All of us children who are still at home think continually of our friends and relations who have gone overseas – who have travelled thousands of miles to find a wartime home and

a kindly welcome in Canada, Australia, New Zealand, South Africa and the United States of America.

My sister and I feel we know quite a lot about these countries. Our father and mother have so often talked to us of their visits to different parts of the world. So it is not difficult for us to picture the sort of life you are all leading, and to think of all the new sights you must be seeing, and the adventures you must be having. But I am sure that you, too, are often thinking of the Old Country.

I know you won't forget us; it is just because we are not forgetting you that I want, on behalf of all the children at home, to send you our love and best wishes – to you and to your kind hosts as well. Before I finish I can truthfully say to you all that we children at home are full of cheerfulness and courage. We are trying to do all we can to help our gallant sailors, soldiers and airmen, and we are trying, too, to bear our own share of the danger and sadness of war.

We know, every one of us, that in the end all will be well; for God will care for us and give us

victory and peace. And when peace comes, remember it will be for us, the children of today, to make the world of tomorrow a better and happier place.

My sister is by my side and we are both going to say goodnight to you.

Come on, Margaret.
Goodnight, children.
Goodnight, and good luck to you all."

Princess Elizabeth
Radio address
October 13, 1940

Princess Elizabeth (left) and Princess Margaret in costume for the 1943 Windsor Castle wartime production of the pantomime Aladdin. Elizabeth had the role of Principal Boy while Margaret played Princess of China. Christmas pantomimes took place at Windsor during the Second World War years of 1941-1944 and the two princesses had leading roles. The productions were staged in the Waterloo Chamber in front of enthusiastic audiences, and were written and produced by Windsor Great Park Royal School headmaster Hubert Tannar. The cast also comprised local children, evacuees and friends of the princesses with occasional help from service personnel. An admission charge raised money for the Wool Fund, to supply knitting wool for the making of comforters for the armed forces.

Princess Elizabeth inspecting paratroopers dropping out of the skies during the run-up to D-Day in May 1944.

Princess Elizabeth – on the right – with her sister Princess Margaret in the garden of their wartime residence Windsor Castle in 1941. With the need to save petrol, the sisters' pony-cart has been brought into use.

Princesses Elizabeth and Margaret sign the first ever wartime savings certificates as they are made available to the public in January 1943.

During her 16th birthday parade on April 21, 1942, Princess Elizabeth shakes hands with the officers of the Grenadier Guards at Windsor Castle.

Princesses Elizabeth and Margaret chat with a land girl on the farm of Sandringham House during a visit there on August 22, 1943.

Senior and junior non-commissioned officers stop for a photograph at No 1 MT Training Centre at Camberly in Surrey in 1945. Princess Elizabeth sits at the centre of the back row.

As part of her service, Princess Elizabeth received vehicle maintenance training and learned how to drive. She is pictured working on an Austin 10 light utility vehicle, 1945.

Princess Elizabeth at work with the Auxiliary Territorial Service in April 1945.

Prime Minister Winston Churchill – centre – joins the royal family on the Buckingham Palace balcony for VE Day on May 8, 1945. Amanda Parks/AP/Press Association Images

Princess Elizabeth and the Duke of Edinburgh walk between rows of British war veterans lining a temporary barrier along the Rue D'Aguesseau in Paris as they return from the city's British Embassy, May 16, 1948.

King George VI and Princess Elizabeth talk to liberated United Kingdom and Empire prisoners of war at Buckingham Palace's Empire Day Garden Party, May 24, 1945.

Princess Elizabeth rides in the uniform of a colonel of the Grenadier Guards on the return journey to Buckingham Palace during the Trooping the Colour ceremony at the Horse Guards Parade, June 9, 1949.

In a rare 1940s colour photograph, Princess Elizabeth is joined on stage by the governor of the Royal Hospital, Major General Sir Clive Liddell, during an inspection of the Chelsea Pensioners at the hospital on May 29, 1947.

An informal and private moment between King George VI and Princess Elizabeth is captured during the 1947 royal tour of South Africa. During the visit, the princess recorded a 21st birthday address to the Commonwealth in which she dedicated herself to her subjects.

A princess comes of age… The war is over and Princess Elizabeth is a 22-year-old woman whose actions during the conflict have made her a much-loved member of the royal family. She is pictured arriving to open a church army hotel for young women in London, May 5, 1948.

Wolverhampton Wanderers captain Billy Wright is presented with the FA Cup trophy by Princess Elizabeth following his team's three-goals-to-one win over Leicester City during the cup final at Wembley Stadium on April 30, 1949.

Now 23 years old and married to the Duke of Edinburgh, Princess Elizabeth watches her husband play village cricket in Kent for Mersham against neighbouring Aldington on July 30, 1949. The duke's batting innings was short-lived – out leg-before-wicket to the first ball he faced – but he did take two wickets when bowling. Watching with the princess is Lady Brabourne whose husband is playing wicketkeeper for Mersham.

The Queen and Prince Philip

Prince Philip of Greece and Denmark was born on the island of Corfu on June 10, 1921, becoming a prominent member of the Greek royal family. A little over a year later, his uncle King Constantine I of Greece was forced to abdicate the throne following a military coup and his father Prince Andrew was subsequently banished from Greece for life meaning a young Prince Philip grew up in Saint-Cloud, a suburb of Paris.

With family ties in the UK through his maternal grandfather, Prince Philip attended Cheam School in Hampshire as a child but he was soon relocated to Germany and continued his education there. The rise of the Nazi party saw him move schools again, this time to Scotland, but many of his family members – including his four sisters – remained and the siblings married into German aristocratic circles. This would create controversy later in his life.

In 1939, Prince Philip began a military career, attending the Royal Naval College in Dartmouth. He would later serve in the British Navy in the Second World War. During Prince Philip's first year at the college, King George VI and Queen Consort Queen Elizabeth toured the facility and as distant cousins of the pair, the royal couple asked him to escort Princesses Elizabeth and Margaret. The two had met before at weddings of members of European households, but it was during the Royal Naval College trip that a 13-year-old Princess

Elizabeth first became smitten with Prince Philip and the two began exchanging letters – a practice that would continue throughout the war years.

During that time Princess Elizabeth had come of age and by 1945 was a 19-year-old woman ready to pursue her romantic interest and start a family of her own. In the summer of 1946, Prince Philip asked King George VI for his daughter's hand in marriage – a request which was granted on the condition that any formal engagement be delayed until the following year once Princess Elizabeth had turned 21.

On July 10, 1947, the intended union was officially announced and later that year, on November 20, the two were married at Westminster Abbey in a ceremony broadcast throughout the world on radio. With the nation and empire still recovering from the ravages of war, the event was a relatively simple affair.

Ahead of the nuptials, Prince Philip renounced his Greek and Danish titles, converted from Greek Orthodoxy to Anglicanism and adopted the name Lieutenant Philip Mountbatten taking the surname of his mother's British family. The day before the wedding, he was given the style of His Royal Highness and on the morning of November 20 he was made the Duke of Edinburgh.

Following the ascension of Queen Elizabeth II in 1952, the Duke of Edinburgh became royal consort and has fulfilled duties in this role ever since, appearing with Her Majesty in an official capacity at royal and state events. Alongside his role as consort, he has also been involved with hundreds of charity organisations including serving as president, international president and president emeritus of the World Wildlife Fund.

While making a speech on the occasion of her Diamond Jubilee in 2012, Queen Elizabeth II described the Duke of Edinburgh as her "constant strength and guide" and despite the pressures of the monarchy – and unlike other members of their immediate family – the royal couple have enjoyed a long and happy marriage, free of controversy and public speculation.

Two pictures 60 years apart show Princess Elizabeth and Lieutenant Philip Mountbatten in 1947 on the day of their engagement, and Queen Elizabeth II and the Duke of Edinburgh in 2007 at Broadlands Estates. 2007 photograph Fiona Hanson/PA Archive/PA Images

Princess Elizabeth and the Duke of Edinburgh leave Westminster Abbey as a married couple following their wedding on November 20, 1947.

Londoners surge around the gates of Buckingham Palace to catch a glimpse of Princess Elizabeth and her new fiancé Lieutenant Philip Mountbatten as they acknowledge cheers from the balcony.

A royal gathering at the royal wedding… Princess Elizabeth and her new husband the Duke of Edinburgh pose with guests from UK and European royal households at Buckingham Palace on November 20, 1947.

In the White Drawing Room of Buckingham Palace, the newly engaged Princess Elizabeth and Lieutenant Philip Mountbatten (left) stand alongside Queen Consort Queen Elizabeth, King George VI and Princess Margaret in 1947. The photo was arranged to mark the upcoming royal wedding which would take place in November.

The scene at Westminster Abbey during the wedding service of Princess Elizabeth and the Duke of Edinburgh as the bridegroom places the ring on the finger of the bride in front of Dr Geoffrey Francis Fisher, Archbishop of Canterbury, who solemnised the marriage, November 20, 1947.

At the Royal Windsor Horse Show at Windsor Castle, Princess Elizabeth and the Duke of Edinburgh enjoy proceedings in the company of the show's chairman Geoffrey Cross (left) and its president the Earl of Gowrie (right) on May 12, 1949.

The children of Queen Elizabeth II and the Duke of Edinburgh

Charles, Prince of Wales
BORN: November 14, 1948
Charles is the eldest child of Queen Elizabeth II and the Duke of Edinburgh and remains the heir apparent to the throne of the United Kingdom – the longest-serving British history. Alongside his royal duties - which have become more and more frequent - he is involved with several charitable causes, particularly those concerned with the environment.
New Zealand Defence Force *

Anne, Princess Royal
BORN: August 15, 1950
Anne is the only daughter of Queen Elizabeth II and the Duke of Edinburgh. Aside from her royal engagements she is best known for her equestrian talents, having won medals at the European Eventing Championships in 1971 and 1975 as well as being the first member of the British royal family to compete at the Olympic Games in 1976 in Montreal.
Chatham House *

Prince Andrew, Duke of York
BORN: February 19, 1960
Andrew was the first child born to a reigning monarch since Queen Victoria was on the throne. He holds the rank of commander in the Royal Navy, and served as an active duty helicopter pilot during the Falklands conflict, flying on multiple missions including anti-surface warfare and casualty evacuation.
Aaron McCracken/Harrisons/Northern Ireland Office *

Prince Edward, Earl of Wessex
BORN: March 10, 1964
Edward is the youngest child of Queen Elizabeth II and the Duke of Edinburgh. As his father has taken steps back from public life, Edward has taken on several of his duties including acting as the president of the Commonwealth Games Federation and attending Gold Award ceremonies for the Duke of Edinburgh Awards.
MT Hurson/Harrisons/Northern Ireland Office *

The newborn Prince Charles sleeps in the arms of his mother after his christening at Buckingham Palace while King George VI, the Duke of Edinburgh and Queen Consort Queen Elizabeth look on, December 15, 1948.

Princess Elizabeth watches over her baby son at Buckingham Palace on December 23, 1948.

The Duke of Edinburgh holds the newest addition to the royal family, Princess Anne, on the lawn at Clarence House on August 8, 1951. Princess Elizabeth and Prince Charles join the royal family photo.

Brother and sister Prince Charles and Princess Anne enjoy being pushed on the swings as Queen Elizabeth II and the Duke of Edinburgh spend an autumn afternoon with their children at Balmoral in September 1955.

Prince Andrew, the royal family's latest addition, sits in the Duke of Edinburgh's lap with Queen Elizabeth II, Prince Charles and Princess Anne seated around them on a tartan rug in the grounds of Balmoral.

On the occasion of Her Majesty's 39th birthday, Queen Elizabeth II and the Duke of Edinburgh stand on the steps of Frogmore House at Windsor surrounded by their children Prince Charles, Princess Anne, Prince Andrew and the newest arrival, Prince Edward.

Supportive wife Queen Elizabeth II chats with her polo-playing husband the Duke of Edinburgh at Smith's Lawn, Windsor Great Park on May 6, 1956. Prince Charles and Princess Anne stand alongside, with Her Majesty holding the lead of one of the famous royal Corgis.

Princess Elizabeth and the Duke of Edinburgh stand proudly alongside the royal family as they enjoy a Balmoral holiday in 1951. The couple are joined by Princess Margaret, Queen Consort Queen Elizabeth, King George VI, a baby Princess Anne and a young Prince Charles who can't resist dipping his hand in the water of the ornamental pond.

Arriving at the Portuguese Embassy in London's Belgrave Square on October 26, 1955, Queen Elizabeth II and the Duke of Edinburgh smile as crowds surround their car ahead of a dinner given in their honour by the visiting Portuguese president. As a beautiful young Queen and a charming, handsome consort, the royal couple are among the most recognisable and stylish figures in a world ever more focused on celebrity.

For many years, Queen Elizabeth II and the Duke of Edinburgh insisted on playing a central role in royal ceremonies and pageants and there they are seen at Buckingham Palace after the Trooping the Colour on their horses Burmese and Bachelor Gay respectively on June 1, 1972.

Just as they did in 1947, Queen Elizabeth II and the Duke of Edinburgh walk down the aisle at Westminster Abbey after their Silver Wedding Thanksgiving Service on November 20, 1972. Among those behind are Queen Consort Queen Elizabeth, Prince Charles, Princess Anne, Prince Andrew and Prince Edward.

Queen Elizabeth II and the Duke of Edinburgh are pictured during their traditional summer break at Balmoral on September 26, 1976. The royal couple are seen reading an edition of the *Sunday Times* while petting Tinker, a Corgi/long-haired Dachshund cross. In the background is a painting of Her Majesty's great-great-grandmother Queen Victoria with her Scottish servant John Brown.

A day out at the races has long been a favourite pastime of Queen Elizabeth II and the Duke of Edinburgh and they are pictured at Ascot on June 19, 1962, and then June 18, 2014, as they take a traditional open carriage ride around the track. The royal connection to racing goes back several generations, and Her Majesty inherited several thoroughbred horses on the death of her father King George VI. Despite not gambling, it is said that she is an avid reader of the *Racing Post* and maintains a strong interest in the breeding industry. 2014 photograph David Davies/PA Archive/PA Images

The royal couple have made multiple state visits during their engagement and marriage, and Queen Elizabeth II and the Duke of Edinburgh are pictured standing at the Bedaling Pass – 50 miles north west of Beijing – on the Great Wall of China during the third day of a trip to the country, October 14, 1986. Ron Bell/PA Archive/PA Images

Wearing formal attire at an official reception in Papua New Guinea, Queen Elizabeth II and the Duke of Edinburgh share a moment of conversation, October 1982. Anwar Hussein/EMPICS Entertainment

Queen Elizabeth II and the Duke of Edinburgh inspect the floral tributes left at Buckingham Palace following the death of Princess Diana, September 5, 1997. John Stillwell/PA Archive/PA Images

The royal couple had shared more than half of the 20th
century as husband and wife when they saw in the year 2000
with a raised glass as the clock strikes midnight on New Year's
Day during the celebrations to mark the opening of the
Millennium Dome in London. Pictured to the right of Queen
Elizabeth II and the Duke of Edinburgh is Prime Minister Tony
Blair. Fiona Hanson/PA Archive/PA Images

Queen Elizabeth II and the Duke of Edinburgh leave St Paul's
Cathedral together on March 13, 2015, following a service to
mark the end of British combat operations in Afghanistan
which had begun in the wake of the September 11 terrorist
attacks in New York, Washington and rural Pennsylvania.
Steve Parsons/PA Archive/PA Images

Queen Elizabeth II and the Duke of Edinburgh
are given a guided tour of the set of popular
soap opera Eastenders on November 28, 2001.
Her Majesty's tour guide is actress Barbara
Windsor who plays Peggy Mitchell (right), while
Prince Philip is accompanied by Wendy Richard,
aka Pauline Fowler. The four are standing
outside the programme's iconic Queen Vic pub
which stands in Albert Square – fictional
locations named after Queen Elizabeth's great-
great-grandparents Queen Victoria and her
consort Prince Albert. Michael Stephens/PA
Archive/PA Images

In full regal attire, Queen Elizabeth II and the
Duke of Edinburgh preside over the House of
Lords prior to Her Majesty's speech at the 2004
State Opening of Parliament. PA/ROTA/PA
Archive/PA Images

The 1950s

The Second World War had ended five years before, yet as the 1950s dawned the effects were still being felt across the UK as an age of austerity continued. Great Britain was a nation in need of a lift, and it came in June 1953 as Queen Elizabeth II was crowned during a coronation ceremony watched on television by an estimated 20 million Britons.

On February 6 the year before, Princess Elizabeth had ascended to the throne following the death of her father King George VI. Popular among his subjects across the world after his leadership during the war years, the King's passing was met with grief but it also drew a line under those years of hardship. The death of Queen Consort Queen Mary, grandmother of Her Majesty and wife of King George V on March 24, 1953, further laid to rest those links to the past.

Britain had a new young leader who would embrace the challenges of the second half of the 20th century and while the next generation would never forget the sacrifices made it could move forward and consign the war to the annals of history. On June 2, 1953, Her Majesty's coronation captured the changing mood.

Pomp and pageantry was the order of the day for the public and the jubilation was heightened even further as news broke that New Zealander Edmund Hillary had become the first man to scale Mount Everest. Suddenly anything seemed possible.

A year later, in May 1954, 25-year-old London medical student Roger Bannister became the first person in the world to run a mile in under four minutes – a feat that was yet another shot in the arm for the nation. Sparked by the coronation and sustained by more and more live sport, sales of television sets rocketed throughout the remaining years of the decade and the new medium began to take its place at the centre of people's daily lives.

Car ownership increased too and so whether through a TV screen or under the power of four wheels, British people began to see more of their own country and the rest of the world than ever before. These facets of British life, being so new, were not something any monarch had ever had to contend with before.

The challenges facing Queen Elizabeth II weren't just cultural however, as 1956 saw the onset of the Suez Crisis. In October, Israel invaded the Egyptian Sinai and was swiftly followed by Great Britain and France – a response to the Egyptian nationalisation of the Suez Canal. Egyptian forces were quickly defeated but, because of the impact that the conflict had on the ability of international vessels to pass through the vital trade route, and the fear of Soviet involvement, American President Dwight D Eisenhower compelled the UK and France to withdraw.

Prime Minister Anthony Eden was forced to resign as it became clear Britain was no longer able to exert its influence without the co-operation of its most powerful ally. Queen Elizabeth II now had the reputation of a country to rebuild.

Setting foot on British soil for the first time since her accession, Queen Elizabeth II disembarks after her night flight from Kenya. Her Commonwealth trip was cut short when she learned of the death of King George VI.

Queen Elizabeth II sits under an umbrella in heavy rain at the unveiling of the memorial statue to her father King George VI at the Carlton Garden in London on October 21, 1955. In the background facing her are the Duke and Duchess of Gloucester.

The royal family watch the Grand National from the top of the grandstand at Aintree racecourse in Liverpool on March 25, 1950. This was the 104th running of the race and nearly half a million people packed in to the venue for this first 'royal' National since the end of the Second World War. Queen Consort Queen Elizabeth and her daughter jointly owned second-favourite Monaveen and their runner was well-placed until a mistake at The Chair nearly unseated the jockey. The race was won by 10/1 shot Freebooter ridden by Irish jockey Jimmy Power. Queen Consort Queen Elizabeth stands on the front row, third from left, with King George VI to her left Princess Elizabeth next to him and Princess Margaret second from the right.

Princess Elizabeth fusses over one the royal Corgis on September 21, 1950.

A two-year-old Prince Charles watches the procession of Queen Juliana of Holland with his mother as it moves to Guildhall from Buckingham Palace during a state visit to Britain on November 22, 1950.

Princess Elizabeth had to deputise for her ailing father during the early 1950s, in this instance presenting the King's Colour to the Royal Air Force at a parade of 2500 RAF personnel in Hyde Park on May 26, 1951.

The "closest and most friendly relations" with the USA was among Queen Elizabeth II's commitments as she spoke to a joint session of the House of Lords and House of Commons at the opening of Parliament on November 4, 1952. Her Majesty arrived in a royal carriage looking regal in a crown-like tiara.

Prince Charles, aged four, looking out of a Buckingham Palace window on the day of his mother's coronation, June 2, 1953. National Media Museum *

Queen Elizabeth II and the Duke of Edinburgh arrive at Westminster Abbey to take part in the traditional Royal Maundy Service on April 10, 1952 – Her Majesty's first public engagement since the beginning of her reign.

Princess chooses royal family over love

Princess Margaret first met Group Captain Peter Townsend when he was equerry to King George VI – and at the time he was married with two children. Captain Townsend later separated from his wife and the two became romantically involved.

The relationship was kept out of the press for many years, but at Queen Elizabeth II's coronation her younger sister let slip a gesture of familiar affection when she brushed some fluff from Captain Townsend's jacket and the news finally broke.

Her Majesty was aware of the couple's intention to marry but had asked them to wait until after the coronation before moving ahead with their plans.

In the 1950s, marrying a divorcee was still viewed with considerable disapproval and went against the church's stance that Christian marriage should never be dissolved.

Once she had turned 25, Princess Margaret needed the consent of Parliament to marry and knowing that the government would never approve she knew that going ahead with the union would mean renouncing her title and any financial income which went with it – just as her uncle Edward VIII had done when he gave up the throne for the American Wallis Simpson.

On October 31, 1955, she issued a statement through the press announcing that she would not be pursuing a marriage. She said: "I have reached this decision entirely alone, and in doing so I have been strengthened by the unfailing support and devotion of Group Captain Townsend." Princess Margaret would go on to marry photographer Anthony Armstrong-Jones in 1960.

Ethiopia's Emperor Haile Selassie acknowledges crowds as he arrives at Buckingham Palace with Queen Elizabeth II at the head of a state precession on October 14, 1954. The African ruler was met by Her Majesty at Victoria Station and they rode side-by-side to the royal residence in a gilded royal coach. This was the emperor's first trip to London since being exiled from his home country by Italian dictator Benito Mussolini in the 1930s.

The runners and riders for the 1954 Epsom Derby parade before the race as Queen Elizabeth II and The Queen Mother discuss the chances of Her Majesty's horse Landau. Never Say Die became the first American colt to win the race in 73 years, ridden by Lester Piggott.

From left to right: Princess Ragnhild of Norway, Queen Elizabeth II and Princess Astrid, also of Norway at the Royal Palace in Oslo during Her Majesty's state visit to the country in June 1955.

Family time for Queen Elizabeth II as she helps five-year-old daughter Princess Anne – a future Olympic equestrian medal winner – to adjust the bridle of Greensleeves the pony in the grounds of Balmoral, September 18, 1955. Barratts/S&G Barratts/EMPICS Archive

At the 1956 Stockholm Equestrian Games, Queen Elizabeth II gasps as a mount slips during the dressage section – Princess Margaret also looks on with cigarette holder in hand. The royal sisters visited the event on June 12 following a state visit to Sweden.

The Tower of London's Yeomen Warders – popularly known as the Beefeaters – form a guard of honour for Queen Elizabeth II as she leaves Westminster Abbey following the annual Royal Maundy Service on March 29, 1956. The traditional event sees the ruling monarch distribute Maundy money every Easter in recognition of the service of elderly people to their community and church. Usually taking place in London, Her Majesty decided early in her reign to hold the event at different venues each year and it has taken place at cathedrals throughout the UK since. There have only been four occasions during that time when Queen Elizabeth II has not presented the Maundy money herself.

Beauchamp Oxford Lady – a Jersey cow – appears unimpressed by her new royal status having been given as a gift to Queen Elizabeth II on July 24, 1957. Her Majesty shares a joke with the Duke of Edinburgh as she's presented with the animal at the Jersey Agricultural and Horticultural Society Show, which the royal couple visited on the first day of a Channel Islands tour.

French president René Coty chats with Queen Elizabeth II during a reception in honour of the monarch at the Louvre Museum in Paris on April 10, 1957. The event – held on the third day of Her Majesty's state visit to France – was hosted by Prime Minster Guy Mollet and the French government.

Speaking from the Bristol exchange, Queen Elizabeth II makes Britain's first trunk dialled telephone call on December 5, 1958. The new technology allows users to make long-distance calls directly, rather than having to be connected by an operator. Her Majesty made the call to Edinburgh and spoke to the Lord Provost.

Ticker tape and confetti float down from the high-rise buildings of Manhattan as Queen Elizabeth II and the Duke of Edinburgh travel in a bubble-domed car up Broadway to City Hall during a visit to New York on October 21, 1957. Thousands of Americans packed on to the city's sidewalks, some waving British flags, to catch a glimpse of the monarch passing by. On the same day, Her Majesty delivered a speech to the United Nations General Assembly in her role as Commonwealth leader.

The Royal Train departs Weymouth on April 29, 1959, with Prince Charles and Queen Elizabeth II on board. The 10-year-old prince and his mother were on their way to inspect aircraft carrier HMS *Eagle*.

Queen Elizabeth II escorts visiting US President Dwight D Eisenhower through two rows of the Royal Highland Fusiliers at the gates of Balmoral Castle on August 28, 1959. The American head of state had flown to London as Her Majesty's guest before making the trip to Scotland.

Miners at Rothes Colliery in Scotland look on as Queen Elizabeth II dons white overalls, scarf, helmet and black gumboots to make her first visit to a coal mine on July 1, 1958. Her Majesty spent half an hour underground getting a taste of life at the coal face.

Three-year-old Charles Early presents Queen Elizabeth II with a blue blanket from his father's factory, a gift for Prince Charles, on April 8, 1959. Her Majesty was visiting Witney in Oxfordshire, famous for the manufacture of blankets, gloves and other woollen goods.

The 1960s

The 1960s was a time of great change for the world, and Great Britain was no exception. Much of the cultural shift carried echoes of what was happening across the Atlantic Ocean where – eight years after a young and stylish leader had captured the imagination in the UK – John F Kennedy's presidential victory had revitalised the USA.

A sense of new beginnings had allowed Britain to move on from the Suez Crisis and Queen Elizabeth II played a vital role in re-establishing her country's place in the world, becoming an international stateswoman.

Both at home and abroad, Her Majesty had to maintain political neutrality, but she was still able to make her mark and embarked on a number of historic international visits during the decade. Following her trip to New York in 1957 when she had delivered a speech to the United Nations, Her Majesty continued to pursue improved international diplomacy and in 1965 became the first British monarch to enter Berlin since before the outbreak of the First World War.

Improved relations abroad and increased freedom at home were cause for hope, but the 1960s also saw a series of events which rocked the country. In 1963, US President John F Kennedy was shot and killed by an assassin while visiting Texas and a world – including those in the UK – went into mourning. The shocking death – coming just a year after the Cuban Missile Crisis had brought the USA and Soviet Union to the brink of nuclear war – was a stark reminder of the fragile nature of global affairs.

Domestically, the continued prominence of TV meant interest in the royal family was greater than ever and reporters, photographers and video recorders followed Her Majesty across the globe. The first TV programme about the family life of the royal household was made in 1969, and it aired to an audience of 23 million.

Also garnering a large TV audience was the ceremony held to mark the Investiture of Prince Charles as Prince of Wales at Caernarfon Castle. Officially, the title was granted to Her Majesty's eldest child by Letters Patent on July 26, 1958, but it wasn't until July 1969 – when Prince Charles was 20 – that a formal ceremony took place with Queen Elizabeth II explaining that she wanted to ensure her son was old enough to fully understand the significance of the event. In preparation, Prince Charles had spent several weeks studying Welsh history and culture as well as learning the Welsh language itself so he could reply during the proceedings in two languages.

By the time the decade came to a close, Great Britain's international affairs had stabilised and all was relatively calm at home. The time had come then for attention to turn to the Commonwealth and the 1970s would see Queen Elizabeth II make a series of visits to her subjects living across the world.

At Green Park underground station, Queen Elizabeth II inspects the driver's cab of a London tube train during the opening of a new section of the Victoria Line on March 7, 1969.

The Mayor of West Berlin, Willy Brandt, talks with Queen Elizabeth II as the pair stand in front of the West German capital's City Hall, May 27, 1965.

The stylish and glamorous Queen Elizabeth II during a garden party in the grounds of the Royal Hospital Chelsea on June 1, 1967.

Queen Elizabeth II with Commonwealth leaders at the 10th Commonwealth Prime Ministers' Conference in 1960. This event was held at Windsor Castle with one of the key concerns on the agenda being the ongoing issue of apartheid in South Africa. On the front row, from left to right, are EJ Cooray, justice minister of Ceylon, New Zealand Prime Minister Walter Nash, India's Prime Minister Jawaharlal Nehru, Queen Elizabeth II, Canadian Prime Minister John Diefenbaker, Australian Prime Minister Robert Menzies and South Africa's Minister of External Affairs Eric Louw. On the back row, left to right, are Tunku Abdul Rahman, Prime Minister of British Malaya, Federation of Rhodesia and Nyasaland Prime Minister Roy Welensky, British Prime Minister Harold Macmillan, Pakistan's President Ayub Khan and Kwame Nkrumah, the president of Ghana.

The Queen's Cup polo competition has long been a favourite of Her Majesty, and here she presents a medal to Centaurs team member JJ Lucas on June 12, 1960.

Queen Elizabeth II arrives at Earls Court on June 30, 1960, to attend a performance of the Royal Tournament – the world's largest military tattoo and pageant held annually by the British Armed Forces from 1880 to 1999.

Royal photographers capture a more informal moment as Queen Elizabeth II uses her own camera in Nepal, February 26, 1961.

Striking evidence of how international relationships have changed during the reign of Queen Elizabeth II as Her Majesty is pictured with the Shah of Persia in Iran during a parade of troops, March 1961.

Queen Elizabeth II pulls the lever to launch Great Britain's first nuclear-powered submarine, HMS Dreadnought. The event, at the Vickers-Armstrong yard at Barrow-in-Furness, took place on Trafalgar Day – October 21, 1960 – the 155th anniversary of the Battle of Trafalgar.

The Duke of Edinburgh and Queen Elizabeth II host a Queen's Dinner at Buckingham Palace for US President John F Kennedy and his wife Jacqueline Kennedy on June 5, 1961. US government/John F Kennedy Presidential Library and Museum, Boston

Members of the royal family and the relatives of John F Kennedy stand together in silence on May 14, 1965, at a memorial dedicated to the late American president at Runnymede in Surrey – the location where King John agreed the Magna Carta. The sombre event includes a touching moment as the Duke of Edinburgh holds the hand of John Kennedy Jr. In the front row, left to right: Queen Elizabeth II (who dedicated the memorial), Lord Harlech (ambassador to the USA and chairman of the Kennedy Memorial Trustees), Caroline Kennedy, Jacqueline Kennedy, John Kennedy Jr, the Duke of Edinburgh. In the back row, left to right: Patricia Lawford-Kennedy, Senator Robert Kennedy, Joan Bennet Kennedy, Senator Edward Kennedy.

Prince Charles inspects the animals at the Severn Wildfowl Trust in Slimbridge, Gloucestershire, as his parents Queen Elizabeth II, the Duke of Edinburgh and trust director Peter Scott look on, April 22, 1961.

At the Badminton Horse Trials on April 13, 1962, Princess Anne and Queen Elizabeth II take a close look at the programme as they sit with Princess Margaret, the Duke of Beaufort, The Queen Mother and Princess Mary.

Holiday camp king Sir Billy Butlin gives Queen Elizabeth II and the Duke of Edinburgh a tour of his site in Pwllheli, North Wales, on August 10, 1963.

Actor Peter O'Toole and director David Lean talk with Queen Elizabeth II at the world premiere of Lawrence of Arabia in Leicester Square, London, on December 10, 1962.

Ahead of the Royal Variety Performance at the London Palladium, Queen Elizabeth II talks to actress and singer Gracie Fields, November 2, 1964.

Queen Elizabeth II is surrounded by members of the Women's Institute from across Britain during a garden party at Buckingham Palace on May 31, 1965.

Prince Charles and The Queen Mother follow Queen Elizabeth II and the Duke of Edinburgh during the funeral service for Sir Winston Churchill at St Paul's Cathedral on January 30, 1965. The state funeral was considered to be the largest of its kind to have been held anywhere in the world up until that time.

At Epsom racecourse in Surrey, Queen Elizabeth II shares a private joke with her stable trainer Captain Cecil Boyd-Rochfort on June 2, 1965.

Comedian Ken Dodd is presented to Queen Elizabeth II at the Royal Variety Performance at London Palladium on November 9, 1965. Also pictured from left to right either side of Dodd are Max Bygraves, Spike Milligan and Dudley Moore.

England captain Bobby Moore holds the Jules Rimet Trophy following his side's four-two victory over West Germany in football's 1966 World Cup Final on July 30. The winners were the host nation, which meant Queen Elizabeth II could present the honour at Wembley Stadium after seeing the English squad triumph in a thrilling match which concluded with Kenneth Wolstenholme's famous line: "They think it's all over... it is now." Standing behind Moore waiting to greet Her Majesty is Geoff Hurst who had scored a hat-trick in the match, still the only player to achieve the feat in a World Cup Final.

Sir Laurence Olivier introduces Queen Elizabeth II to Maggie Smith as Her Majesty attends the charity premiere of Othello at the Odeon in Leicester Square, London, May 2, 1966.

By the end of the 1960s the royal family had grown to include Prince Andrew and Prince Edward. The youngsters join older siblings Princess Anne and Prince Charles on Her Majesty's 42nd birthday – along with their parents – during a walk in the grounds of Frogmore House in Windsor.

Seen from the opposite bank is the new *Queen Elizabeth 2* ocean liner stretching across the River Clyde following an official launch by Her Majesty, September 20, 1967.

Queen Elizabeth II crowns her son as Charles, Prince of Wales, during his investiture at Caernarfon Castle, July 1, 1969.

Having become the first man to step onto the surface of the moon on July 21, 1969, Neil Armstrong and his fellow crew members from Apollo 11 embarked on a triumphant world tour. The astronaut is pictured talking to Queen Elizabeth II and Prince Andrew at Buckingham Palace on October 14 in between his wife Janet Armstrong (right) and Pat Collins (left), wife of Michael Collins.

The Queen and the Commonwealth

Alongside her role as UK monarch, Queen Elizabeth II is also recognised as the head of the Commonwealth. The concept of the Commonwealth originated in the mid-20th century as a number of the countries which made up the British Empire began to seek self-rule. In 1949, the London Declaration formally stated that those nations wishing to govern themselves independently but still remain part of a group would recognise King George VI as head of the Commonwealth. Unlike the constitutional monarchy, succession is not automatic for independent member states so when the King died the Commonwealth leaders had to formally recognise Queen Elizabeth II as next in line; which they duly did.

Member nations have joined and left in the years since, and today the Commonwealth consists of 53 member states. Of these, 16 are Commonwealth realms which recognise Queen Elizabeth II as sovereign head of state – Great Britain is included in this count. The other countries include 32 republics and five nations each with its own monarch.

As the Commonwealth is a voluntary organisation and its members have no legal obligation to each other or to the group as a whole, Her Majesty's role is a symbolically significant and unifying one and she is responsible for ensuring its principles of democracy and the rule of law are upheld and its joint history, culture and language celebrated.

As a princess and in the time since her accession Her Majesty has made many efforts to fulfil this duty and extol the virtues of the Commonwealth, even going to such lengths as ensuring her coronation dress was embroidered with the floral emblems of Commonwealth countries. Her Majesty's primary way of strengthening ties however has been through regular visits to the Commonwealth member nations across the globe.

Since becoming Queen, she has undertaken more than 200 visits to Commonwealth countries and has visited every nation involved with the exception of Cameroon and Rwanda which joined in 1995 and 2009 respectively. In 1953 and 1954, Her Majesty and the Duke of Edinburgh conducted a six-month world tour with the Queen becoming the first reigning monarch of Australia and New Zealand to visit either country.

In 1977, Queen Elizabeth II and the Duke of Edinburgh embarked on another extensive tour of the Commonwealth nations to mark the Silver Jubilee with many further trips following in the 1980s and 90s.

As Her Majesty moved into her 80s, a gruelling work schedule has meant careful management of foreign trips. In October 2011, Queen Elizabeth II made her last trip – to date – to an overseas Commonwealth realm when she attended the Commonwealth Heads of Government Meeting in Australia. On those occasions when she has been absent from official engagements, Prince Charles has fulfilled her duties. Queen Elizabeth II is kept updated with Commonwealth developments through regular contact with the Commonwealth secretary-general who is based at central offices in London. The office coordinates many activities and events including overseeing the Commonwealth Games sporting events.

Princess Elizabeth and the Duke of Edinburgh address the large crowd who turned out to see them in Canada, 1951. Library and Archives Canada *

Princess Elizabeth and the Duke of Edinburgh take a walk in Nova Scotia, Canada, 1951. Library and Archives Canada *

Outside the walls of Old Delhi, India, Queen Elizabeth II addresses a vast gathering of more than 250,000 people at the Ramlila Grounds on January 28, 1961. It was by far the largest audience ever directly addressed by Her Majesty.

Thousands of people gather in and around Rockdale Town Hall in the suburbs of Sydney, Australia, on June 2, 1953, to celebrate the coronation of Queen Elizabeth II. Several outdoor loud-speakers allowed the crowd to listen to the ceremony live on BBC radio which broadcast for an unprecedented seven hours. Australian Photographic Agency/State Library of New South Wales *

A citizen of Calgary, Canada, spreads a blanket for Princess Elizabeth as she steps from a stage coach to attend a rodeo on October 21, 1951.

Aborigines wave flags for Queen Elizabeth II and the Duke of Edinburgh as they drive round Townsville, Queensland, during a tour of Australia, March 13, 1954.

Queen Elizabeth II, wearing the Korowai Cloak which is a symbol of paramount rank, inspects Maoris at a reception held in Her Majesty's honour in Arawa Park, Rotorua, during a royal tour of New Zealand, January 7, 1954.

Four-year-old Mei Kainona bows as she presents a bouquet of native flowers to Queen Elizabeth II in Suva, Fiji, December 17, 1953.

Anne Emmett, wife of a coal corporation chairman, walks with Queen Elizabeth II after leaving a miner's house in Enugu, Nigeria, on February 7, 1956. A gallery full of native children watch as a stray chicken walks across Her Majesty's path.

Australian cricketer Richie Benaud shakes hands with Queen Elizabeth II ahead of the final day's play of the second test of the Ashes on June 25, 1956. The tourists beat England by 185 runs to win the match, but it was England who would capture the series with a two-tests-to-one victory.

As they prepare to lay a wreath at the memorial to the founder of Pakistan Muhammad Ali Jinnah on February 1, 1961, Queen Elizabeth II and the Duke of Edinburgh have their feet covered by attendants. Protocol calls for the covering of feet before anyone can enter hallowed ground.

With Prince Charles and Princess Anne by her side, Queen Elizabeth II passes through crowds at the Royal Easter Show in Sydney, April 3, 1970.

Queen Elizabeth II stands among children at the Moore Park playground in Sydney, March 6, 1963.

Spectators shelter beneath umbrellas, and Queen Elizabeth II and the Duke of Edinburgh do likewise as they are driven in a Land Rover while visiting a school sports carnival at Nathan, Brisbane, Australia on March 10, 1977. Ron Bell/PA Archive/PA Images

Queen Elizabeth II and the Duke of Edinburgh are carried shoulder high in canoes during a trip to Tuvalu, October 26, 1982.

Preparing for a flight back to Great Britain, Queen Elizabeth II inspects a Fijian guard of honour on November 1, 1982.

During a visit to the Solomon Islands on October 1, 1982, Queen Elizabeth II tours the Central Hospital.

Waving to the gathered crowds, Queen Elizabeth II and the Duke of Edinburgh step off the plane at Adelaide Airport, Australia, on February 25, 1992. Jeff Widener/AP/Press Association Images

A large group follow behind Queen Elizabeth II and the Duke of Edinburgh as they arrive at the Mahatma Gandhi memorial – Raj Ghat – in Delhi, India, November 18, 1983. Ron Bell/PA Archive/PA Images

During her first visit to South Africa since 1947, Queen Elizabeth II stands beside President Nelson Mandela after stepping ashore from the Royal Yacht in Cape Town, March 20, 1995. Martin Keene/PA Archive/PA Images

After opening the Bahamas Tourism Training Centre, Queen Elizabeth II inspects the uniforms of trainee chefs and waiters who formed a guard of honour on her departure, March 6, 1994. Martin Keene/PA Archive/PA Images

Following proper protocol by wearing socks and headscarf, Queen Elizabeth II tours the Shah Faisal Mosque in Islamabad, Pakistan, on October 7, 1997. John Stillwell/PA Archive/PA Images

Ghanaian President Jerry Rawlings speaks with Queen Elizabeth II after she addressed the country's Parliament and underlined the importance of democracy in the former West African colony, November 8, 1999. Fiona Hanson/PA Archive/PA Images

At the opening of London's Royal Commonwealth Society Club, Queen Elizabeth II talks with Malaysian candle dancers following their performance during the event on June 4, 1998.

Canadian ice hockey star Markus Naslund talks to Queen Elizabeth II as she holds the puck before starting a game between Naslund's Vancouver Canucks and the San Jose Sharks on October 6, 2002. Her Majesty was on a two-week tour of the country as part of her Golden Jubilee celebrations, and had enjoyed a lunch as the Fairmont Express Hotel where she and the Duke of Edinburgh were greeted by the pipes and drums of the Canadian Scottish Regiment. Kirsty Wigglesworth/PA Archive/PA Images

As part of the Centennial Celebration of the Canadian city of Edmonton at Commonwealth Stadium on May 24, 2005, Queen Elizabeth II and the Duke of Edinburgh cut a cake in the shape of Alberta's legislative building. Premier of Alberta Ralph Klein looks on. Fiona Hanson/PA Archive/PA Images

During her first visit to the country since 1956, Queen Elizabeth II meets locals at a reception at the State Banqueting House in Abuja, Nigeria on December 3, 2003. Kirsty Wigglesworth/PA Archive/PA Images

Two days ahead of the Commonwealth Games in Melbourne, Australia, Queen Elizabeth II receives flowers from waiting schoolchildren after a Commonwealth Day service in Sydney on March 13, 2006. Rob Griffith/AP/Press Association Images

Volunteers from an Australian State Emergency Service meet Queen Elizabeth II on March 14, 2006. Rob Griffith/AP/Press Association Images

Queen Elizabeth II is welcomed to the Toa Payoh housing complex in Singapore as part of a two-day state visit to the former crown colony on March 17, 2006. Ian Jones/Telegraph pool/PA Archive/PA Images

Touring the grounds of Canberra's government house in Australia, Queen Elizabeth II – seated next to the Duke of Edinburgh – views grey kangaroos from a solar powered buggy, October 20, 2011. Rick Rycroft/AP/Press Association Images

At a government building reception in Canberra, Australia, Queen Elizabeth II meets 6ft 8in London-born Australian basketball star Elizabeth Cambage, October 21, 2011. John Stillwell/PA Archive/PA Images

Following a lunch in central London, Queen Elizabeth II stands at the centre of Commonwealth nations' heads of government and other Commonwealth representatives on June 6, 2012. Lefteris Pitarakis/PA Archive/PA Images

On day one of the second Ashes test at Lord's on July 18, 2013, Queen Elizabeth II shakes hands with Australian cricketer Phillip Hughes. Tragedy would strike a little more than a year later when the 25-year-old batsman died on November 27 after being struck in the neck by a delivery at Sydney Cricket Ground. Anthony Devlin/ PA Archive/PA Images

At the Commonwealth War Graves Commission cemetery, Queen Elizabeth II lays a wreath at the foot of the Cross of Sacrifice during a service of remembrance in Normandy, France on June 6, 2014. Jonathan Brady/PA Archive/PA Images

Queen Elizabeth II and the Duke of Edinburgh meet with South Africa's Victor Matfield (left), Australia's Henry Speight (centre) and South Africa's Bryan Habana (right) at a Rugby World Cup reception at Buckingham Palace on October 12, 2015. Dominic Lipinski/PA Wire/Press Association Images

The 1970s

Decolonisation of British imperial territories was in full effect during the 1970s. By the end of the decade, more than 20 countries had gained independence from Great Britain as part of a plan to transition to self-rule; with some remaining part of the Commonwealth.

As the UK's ties to its former empire weakened, the British government tried to establish a leading role closer to home and in 1973 joined the European Economic Community – today known as the European Union.

Unlike the Commonwealth of which Queen Elizabeth II is the head, European issues have always been a UK government issue on which Her Majesty has maintained impartiality. She has, however, spoken on multiple occasions about the dangers of division in Europe and the importance of the relationships Britain enjoys with its closest allies on the continent.

While these international changes were significant, the unpredictability of international affairs had relented from the frantic height of the 1960s – matters at home though were not as simple. In 1970, Edward Heath became prime minister of a Conservative government, promising a 'quiet revolution' that would turn around Britain's economic fortunes.

An energy crisis, financial crash and ongoing miners' strike shattered those aspirations however. Labour's Harold Wilson got the country back to work, but not without a humiliating bailout from the International Monetary Fund. A difficult political decade ended with Jim Callaghan being admonished by the unions during the Winter of Discontent and Britain's first female prime minister, Margaret Thatcher, replacing him in the 1979 General Election. As with Europe, Queen Elizabeth II

was bound by political impartiality and unable to interject. What she could do, however, was rouse her people and in 1977 Her Majesty's Silver Jubilee celebrations did just that as the nation showed the strength of its support for the monarch.

During Commonwealth visits Queen Elizabeth II had made popular the royal walkabouts where she would greet the hundreds and at times thousands of well-wishers who had lined the streets.

On June 7, following the Silver Jubilee service in St Paul's Cathedral, Queen Elizabeth II spent about 40 minutes walking from the venue to Guildhall for her next engagement and spoke with several people along the route. The media hailed Her Majesty as 'the People's Queen'. Earlier in the day 100,000 people had flocked to Buckingham Palace and chanted 'We want the Queen,' which turned to raucous cheers as the royal family appeared on the balcony.

It seemed that the royal family would move into 1980 on a positive note of soaring popularity, but on August 27, 1979, the assassination of one of the royal family's most prominent members would see the decade end in tragedy.

Lord Mountbatten – the uncle of the Duke of Edinburgh – was killed by the IRA when a bomb which had been planted on his boat was detonated. The 79-year-old died from his injuries along with his 14-year-old grandson Nicholas Knatchbull, Lady Brabourne and crewmember Paul Maxwell. Lord Mountbatten received a ceremonial funeral at Westminster Abbey attended by Queen Elizabeth II, the Duke of Edinburgh, members of the royal family and members of other European royal households. The televised service included a reading from Prince Charles.

After opening the new London Bridge, Queen Elizabeth II goes on a royal walkabout across the structure, March 16, 1973.

Queen Elizabeth II and the Duke of Edinburgh stand next to the coffin of Lord Mountbatten during his Westminster Abbey funeral on September 5, 1979.

All smiles on the occasion of her 48th birthday, Queen Elizabeth II is pictured at Windsor Castle on April 21, 1974.

Attending a performance of the British costume drama Anne of the Thousand Days, Queen Elizabeth II talks to David Frost, February 23, 1970.

In Auckland, Queen Elizabeth II reads her speech at the opening of the New Zealand parliament with Prince Charles listening intently, March 12, 1970.

Queen Elizabeth II talks to gathered crowds in the main shopping precinct in Coventry, June 30, 1970.

In a visit to mark the city's 1900th anniversary, Queen Elizabeth II takes a walk through York's Museum Gardens on June 28, 1971.

The Christmas Day broadcast to the Commonwealth is a tradition Queen Elizabeth II has upheld throughout her reign. On December 21, 1970, Her Majesty is pictured in her Buckingham Palace sitting room filming that year's message.

In the middle of the four-man line-up stand Sid James (middle left) and Bruce Forsyth (middle right). The two met Queen Elizabeth II following their participation in the Royal Variety Performance at the London Palladium on November 15, 1971.

Driving through the gates of Buckingham Palace, Queen Elizabeth II and Emperor Hirohito of Japan arrive in an open landau at the start of his four-day state visit to Britain on October 5, 1971. It was the first time the emperor had been to the royal residence in 50 years.

As part of his Royal Navy service, Prince Charles gives his mother a tour of guided-missile destroyer HMS *Norfolk* at Portsmouth on June 30, 1972. The prince is a sub-lieutenant aboard the vessel. He and Her Majesty are joined by 24-year-old Leading Seaman Robert Bell; the three sharing a joke with those behind the camera.

The Queen Mother receives an honorary doctorate from Queen Elizabeth II at the Royal College of Music in South Kensington, London, on December 5, 1973. Mother and daughter were president and patron of the college respectively.

As part of their silver wedding anniversary celebrations, Queen Elizabeth II and the Duke of Edinburgh visited a farm on their Balmoral Estate, September 1, 1972.

British-born American comedian Bob Hope meets Queen Elizabeth II as she attends the Silver Jubilee Royal Variety Gala at the London Palladium on November 21, 1977.

Australian comedian Barry Humphries – as his famous character Dame Edna Everage – meets Queen Elizabeth II as he performs as part of a variety gala performance at Windsor in aid of Her Majesty's Silver Jubilee Appeal, May 29, 1977.

US President Gerald Ford dancing with Queen Elizabeth II during a state dinner held in Her Majesty's honour, July 7, 1976. Gerald R Ford Presidential Library and Museum

Sitting on a traditional Japanese tatami mat, Queen Elizabeth II uses chopsticks to pick up a piece of roasted fish as she dines in a restaurant in the ancient former capital city of Kyoto, May 10, 1975.

Visiting the Queen Elizabeth Country Park in Hampshire on August 2, 1976, Her Majesty takes in the scenic view.

Berlin's Olympic Stadium had been a stage for Adolf Hitler and the Nazis in 1936 and had seen African-American athlete Jesse Owens challenge the dictator's ideas of Aryan supremacy by winning four gold medals in track and field events. Forty-two years later, Queen Elizabeth II was en route to tour the arena during a state visit to West Germany on May 25, 1978. Ron Bell/PA Archive/PA Images

US President Jimmy Carter (middle right) talks to The Queen Mother and Queen Elizabeth II along with Italian Prime Minister Giulio Andreotti and the Duke of Edinburgh in the Blue Drawing Room at Buckingham Palace, May 7, 1977.

Attending a recording of The Good Life at BBC TV studios in Shepherd's Bush, London, Queen Elizabeth II and the Duke of Edinburgh meet the stars on June 8, 1978. The cast, from left to right: Paul Eddington, Penelope Keith, Felicity Kendal, Richard Briers.

During a visit to the Channel Islands, Queen Elizabeth II walks the narrow streets of St Peter Port to meet residents of Guernsey, June 28, 1978. Ron Bell/PA Archive/PA Images

At the Great Children's Party in Hyde Park on May 30, 1979, Queen Elizabeth II politely refuses a portion of a two-mile long sausage from 10-year-old Cub Scout Jamie Cutting. The event – the world's largest ever children's party – was held to mark the International Year of the Child in 1979.

The 1980s

On February 24, 1981, the engagement of Prince Charles and Lady Diana Spencer was announced by Buckingham Palace. The husband and wife to be pose for an official photograph with Lady Diana's engagement ring in full view. Ron Bell/PA Archive/PA Images

It's one of the most memorable moments and iconic images of the 1980s: Princess Diana dances at a White House dinner with actor John Travolta – star of Grease and Saturday Night Fever – as President Reagan and his wife Nancy look on. The princess and her husband, Prince Charles, attracted huge press and public attention during their visit to the USA which began on November 9, 1985. Anwar Hussein/ EMPICS Entertainment

At the start of 1980s there was one burning question that followed the royal family everywhere: when would Prince Charles marry? The prince, due to turn 32 in 1980, was one of the most eligible bachelors in the world and had enjoyed rumoured romances with a number of women but none had resulted in an engagement.

Prince Charles first met Lady Diana Spencer in 1977 during a visit to her home as the guest of her elder sister Lady Sarah Spencer. It wasn't until 1980 however that a romantic relationship was considered – the pair growing closer in the wake of the compassion and support Lady Diana offered following the death of Lord Mountbatten.

The prince invited the 19-year-old on a sailing weekend aboard royal yacht *Britannia*, and soon after he welcomed her to Balmoral Castle in Scotland to meet the royal family – Queen Elizabeth II, the Duke of Edinburgh and The Queen Mother – all of whom approved the blossoming relationship.

After six months of dating, Prince Charles proposed marriage to Lady Diana during a private dinner at Buckingham Palace ahead of her planned trip to Australia. The prince had intended for her to use the three-week break to consider the proposal but she accepted immediately.

Despite the intense public, press and media attention that surrounded the couple, they managed to keep their engagement secret for three weeks before Buckingham Palace issued a statement through the lord chancellor Lord Maclean: "It is with the greatest pleasure that the Queen and the Duke of Edinburgh

announce the betrothal of their beloved son the Prince of Wales to Lady Diana Spencer, daughter of the Earl of Spencer and the Honourable Mrs Shand Kydd."

Like the Coronation and the Silver Jubilee, the wedding of the Prince Charles and Lady Diana Spencer captured the imagination of the country and became a huge public spectacle with crowds of 600,000 people filling the streets of London. A congregation of 3500 people were at St Paul's Cathedral on July 29, 1981, to witness 20-year-old Lady Diana become Diana, Princess of Wales, and a further 750 million are estimated to have watched proceedings on television. After the ceremony, the newlyweds travelled back to Buckingham Palace in an open-topped state carriage, before emerging on the balcony of the royal residence for a public kiss.

The royal wedding was the highlight of the decade, but it was not one without other incident. Six weeks earlier, during the 1981 Trooping the Colour ceremony, Marcus Sarjeant had brandished a gun and fired six shots at the Her Majesty from close range while she rode her horse Burmese down The Mall. Police later discovered the shots were blanks. In 1982, intruder Michael Fagan also managed to get into Her Majesty's bedroom and spend 10 minutes talking with her before the alarm was raised.

In the same year, the Falklands conflict dominated the news and not only did Queen Elizabeth II have to contend with being the head of a nation in conflict but her son Prince Andrew saw active service as a pilot in the Royal Navy. The prince, Queen Elizabeth II's third child – married Sarah Ferguson on July 23, 1986, at Westminster Abbey and on the same day he was made Duke of York.

Problems continued into 1983 when US President Ronald Reagan sanctioned the invasion of Grenada – a Commonwealth realm – without informing Her Majesty despite the close relationship the two had developed on meetings at Windsor Castle and a Californian ranch.

If these incidents had begun to chip away at the gloss that the royal marriage had given to the start of the decade, then events of the late 1980s would shatter it altogether. Newspaper interest in the royals was at fever pitch and a constant stream of reports emerged speculating as to the strained marriages of Queen Elizabeth II's immediate family; most notably the Prince and Princess of Wales. As 1989 came to a close, the couple's separate lives had become public knowledge and rumours swirled that a formal separation was imminent.

The wedding of Prince Charles and Lady Diana Spencer, July 29, 1981

Prince Charles gives a final wave to the crowds alongside his brother Prince Andrew before entering St Paul's Cathedral.

Earl Spencer leads his daughter Lady Diana down the aisle in St Paul's Cathedral.

The new Princess of Wales walks down the aisle with her husband Prince Charles, following their wedding service.

Father of the bride Earl Spencer travels back to Buckingham Palace after the wedding with the groom's mother Queen Elizabeth II.

Sealed with a kiss; Prince Charles and Princess Diana provide the moment everyone has been waiting for on the balcony of Buckingham Palace.

Prince Charles and Princess Diana travel in an open-top carriage back to Buckingham Palace as an excited crowd lines the street to cheer the procession.

Prince Charles and Princess Diana pose for an official wedding photo at Buckingham Palace.

With her beloved Corgis by her side, Queen Elizabeth II walks the Cross Country course during the second day of the Windsor Horse Trials, May 17, 1980.

Queen Elizabeth II and the Duke of Edinburgh participate in a toast during the commissioning ceremony of HMS *Invincible* in Portsmouth on July 11, 1980.

On the newly built set of Granada Television's Coronation Street in Manchester, Queen Elizabeth II and the Duke of Edinburgh meet cast members (from left to right) Jack Howarth, William Roache, Anne Kirkbride, Eileen Derbyshire and Thelma Barlow on May 5, 1982. Ron Bell/PA Archive/PA Images

A sticky moment for Queen Elizabeth II after shaking hands with strongman Geoff Capes following his victory in the caber tossing event at the Braemar Games in Scotland on September 5, 1982. Her Majesty was warned that she'd be unable to remove the resin used by Capes to improve his grip; The Queen Mother, Prince Charles and Princess Diana see the funny side.

In New Delhi, India, Queen Elizabeth II meets Mother Teresa on November 1, 1983.

After attending morning prayers, Queen Elizabeth II smiles for the gathered public as she leaves the Royal Chapel in Windsor Great Park, April 20, 1986. Peter Kemp/AP/Press Association Images

Princess Diana and her mother-in-law Queen Elizabeth II smile to well-wishers outside London's Clarence House on August 4, 1987.

Queen Elizabeth II officially opens the £460 million Thames Barrier at Woolwich on May 8, 1984.

Jockey Lester Piggott readies his mount Theatrical for the Derby at Epsom watched by Princess Anne, The Queen Mother and Queen Elizabeth II on June 3, 1985.

During a private three-day visit to stud farms in Normandy, France, Queen Elizabeth II strokes Tourmalay – a two-year-old piebald belonging to Alec Head (right), May 23, 1987.

On July 6, 1988, during a state visit to the Netherlands, Queen Elizabeth II walks through the Arnhem-Oosterbeek War Cemetery. Many British paratroopers who died during the Second World War lie buried within its grounds. Eric Blom/AP/Press Association

The fallout from the US invasion of Grenada aside, Queen Elizabeth II enjoyed a strong personal relationship with President Ronald Reagan during his time in office and bestowed a knighthood upon him at Buckingham Palace on June 14, 1989. Her Majesty is pictured alongside Mr Reagan and his wife Nancy following the ceremony where he was made an honorary Knight of Grand Cross and the Most Honourable Order of the Bath. Ron Bell/PA Archive/PA Images

By the end of the 1980s the Cold War, which at its height threatened a global nuclear disaster, had thawed. International relations between countries on the two sides of the Iron Curtain resumed and on November 9, 1989, the Berlin Wall fell. Earlier that year, on April 7, Queen Elizabeth II and the Duke of Edinburgh welcomed Soviet President Mikhail Gorbachev and his wife Raisa to London and are seen in the Waterloo Chamber at Windsor Castle.

The Queen and the Royal Family

The House of Windsor is the current royal house of the United Kingdom and the Commonwealth realms, having been founded by King George V on July 17, 1917, to ensure that all British descendants of Queen Victoria and consort Prince Albert bear that surname. The King had changed from the German Saxe-Coburg and Gotha owing mainly to the anti-German sentiment arising from the First World War.

Princess Elizabeth was born into this established royal household, and would soon become its leader. Following the coronation of Queen Elizabeth II in 1952 it was speculated and expected that the name would be changed again to the House of Mountbatten – the surname of the Duke of Edinburgh – but on the advice of Prime Minister Winston Churchill Her Majesty issued a royal proclamation declaring that the title House of Windsor would remain.

Over time, the four children of Queen Elizabeth II and the Duke of Edinburgh have added grandchildren and great-grandchildren to their family tree, although not all of them bear the name Windsor.

Princess Anne was the first of Her Majesty's children to wed, marrying Captain Mark Phillips at Westminster Abbey on November 14, 1973, in a ceremony that was televised around the world to an estimated audience of 100 million. The couple had two children – Peter Phillips, born November 15, 1977, and Zara Phillips,

born May 15, 1981. On the morning of his wedding however, Captain Phillips turned down the offer of an earldom meaning both Peter and Zara Phillips are in the unusual position of being grandchildren of a monarch but not bearing a royal title and not being officially part of the House of Windsor.

The wedding of Prince Charles and Lady Diana Spencer generated greater public interest because the groom was first in line to the throne, and when the new Princess of Wales gave birth to Prince William on June 21, 1982, he became second behind his father in the order of succession. A younger brother to Prince William, Prince Henry – known as Harry – arrived a little more than two years later on September 15, 1984.

The next to marry was Prince Andrew – who became the Duke of York on the day of his wedding – and he and his now former wife the Duchess of York have two children; Princess Beatrice of York, born August 8, 1988, and Princess Eugenie of York, born March 23, 1990.

All three of these marriages of Queen Elizabeth II's children had ended by the time Prince Edward wed Sophie Rhys-Jones on June 19, 1999, at Windsor Castle – Princess Anne having married a second time to Commander Timothy Laurence on December 12, 1992. The Earl and Countess of Wessex – the titles given to Prince Edward and Miss Rhys-Jones once they were husband and wife – also have two children; Lady Louise

Queen Elizabeth II leads the royal family onto the Buckingham Palace balcony after attending Her Majesty's annual birthday parade Trooping the Colour, June 11, 2011. Dominic Lipinski/PA Archive/PA Images

Windsor, born on November 8, 2003, and James, Viscount Severn, born December 17, 2007.

Their arrivals brought the number of Queen Elizabeth II's grandchildren to eight. On December 29, 2010, Savanah Phillips was born to Peter Phillips and his wife Autumn to give Her Majesty a first great-grandchild. Another daughter, Isla Phillips, was born to the couple on March 29, 2012, although neither bore the name Windsor.

To great public excitement, Clarence House announced on November 16, 2010, that Prince William and long-term partner Catherine Middleton were to marry – the prince giving his fiancée the engagement ring which belonged to his mother Princess Diana.

As Prince William was not heir apparent, the wedding – which took place on April 29, 2011, was not a full state occasion although it was declared a public holiday in Great Britain and featured many official ceremonial aspects such as state carriages and roles for the Foot Guards and Household Cavalry. More than one million people lined the streets between Westminster Abbey – the venue for the nuptials – and Buckingham Palace to catch a glimpse of the newlyweds.

The couple, who were made the Duke and Duchess of Cambridge, announced they were expecting their first child in December 2012, and on July 22, 2013, the arrival of Prince George was announced through a press release issued by Buckingham Palace before the customary formal bulletin informing the public of the royal birth was displayed on an easel outside the royal residence.

A future king had been born, the House of Windsor had a new generation and for only the second time in history three direct heirs to the British throne were alive at the same time – the last time being 1894 when Queen Victoria's great-grandson, the future Edward VIII, was born. Public and media reaction was unprecedented.

On January 17, 2014, Zara Tindall – the married name of Zara Phillips – and her English Rugby World Cup-winner husband Mike Tindall welcomed daughter Mia into the world.

Two years on from the birth of Prince George, the Duchess of Cambridge gave birth to a daughter on May 2, 2015, with Queen Elizabeth's fifth great-grandchild being named Charlotte Elizabeth Diana – Princess Charlotte of Cambridge.

Members of the royal family leave St George's Chapel in Windsor after attending the marriage ceremony of Peter Phillips and Autumn Kelly, May 17, 2008. Shaun Curry/PA Archive/PA Images

The royal family pose for the official christening photo of Prince William at Buckingham Palace, August 4, 1982.

Captain Mark Phillips and Princess Anne leaving the west door of Westminster Abbey after their wedding ceremony on November 14, 1973.

Princess Anne stands between her children Peter and Zara Phillips at the Royal Windsor Horse Show at Home Park where her father the Duke of Edinburgh is competing, May 12, 1984.

An 18-month-old Prince William plays in the gardens of Kensington Palace with his parents, Prince Charles and Princess Diana, sitting in the background, December 14, 1983.

Princess Diana being careful to watch her step as she carries the new born Prince Harry out of St Mary's Hospital accompanied by Prince Charles on September 16, 1984.

Zara Phillips holds the hand of her grandmother Queen Elizabeth II with Peter Phillips following behind at the Horse Society Centenary Display at Smith's Lawn, Windsor Great Park on June 17, 1984.

Prince Andrew and his bride the Duchess of York wave to the crowds as they leave Westminster Abbey following their wedding ceremony on July 23, 1986.

The Duchess of York – wife of Prince Andrew – holds her young daughter Princess Beatrice on her shoulders at the Royal Windsor Horse Show, May 11, 1991. Michael Stephens/PA Archive/PA Images

Prince Charles and Princess Diana take their young sons Princes William and Harry for a cycling trip while on holiday in the Scilly Isles, June 1, 1989.

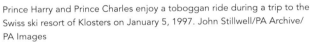

Prince Harry and Prince Charles enjoy a toboggan ride during a trip to the Swiss ski resort of Klosters on January 5, 1997. John Stillwell/PA Archive/PA Images

The Earl of Wessex leaves Frimley Park Hospital with his newborn son James, Viscount Severn, on December 20, 2007. David Parry/PA Archive/PA Images

Princess Eugenie – the daughter of the Duke and Duchess of York – with gifts received from well-wishers following the traditional Christmas Day service at the church on the Sandringham estate, December 25, 1998. Fiona Hanson/PA Archive/PA Images

Prince Andrew accompanies his daughters Princess Eugenie (left) and Princess Beatrice (right) as they arrive at Westminster Abbey for the wedding of Prince William and Catherine Middleton, April 29, 2011. Andrew Milligan/PA Archive/PA Images

Prince William and the Duchess of Cambridge emerge from Westminster Abbey following their wedding ceremony, Prince Harry seen just behind, April 29, 2011. Lewis Whyld/PA Archive/PA Images

Driving himself and new wife the Duchess of Cambridge, Prince William leaves Buckingham Palace for Clarence House on the day of his wedding, April 29, 2011. Chris Ison/PA Archive/PA Images

Mike and Zara Tindall emerge from Canongate Kirk in Edinburgh after their wedding, July 30, 2011. Martin Rickett/PA Archive/PA Images

The Earl and Countess of Wessex with daughter Lady Louise Windsor on their way back to Buckingham Palace during Trooping the Colour on June 11, 2011. Arrow Press /EMPICS Entertainment

Prince Harry from team Invictus tackles Mike Tindall from team Endeavour as they take part in a wheelchair rugby exhibition match at the Copper Box Arena, part of Queen Elizabeth Olympic Park in London, September 12, 2014. Yui Mok/PA Archive/PA Images

Peter and Autumn Phillips ride the carousel at the Royal Windsor Horse Show with their children Savannah Phillips (right) and Isla Phillips (left), May 17, 2014. Steve Parsons/PA Archive/PA Images

It was the photo shared around the world: Prince William and the Duchess of Cambridge leave the Lindo Wing of St Mary's Hospital in London with their newborn son Prince George on July 23, 2013. Dominic Lipinski/PA Archive/PA Images

Princess Anne and her second husband Vice Admiral Sir Timothy Laurence arrive on Chelsea Pier during the Diamond Jubilee River Pageant on the River Thames, June 3, 2012. Bethany Clarke/PA Archive/PA Images

The Duchess of Cornwall, Prince Charles, Prince George, Prince William, the Duchess of Cambridge, Queen Elizabeth II, Prince Harry and James, Viscount Severn, on the balcony of Buckingham Palace following Trooping the Colour at Horse Guards Parade on June 13, 2015. Johnathan Brady/PA Archive/PA Images

Prince William, the Duchess of Cambridge and Prince George walk in the grounds of the Church of St Mary Magdalene in Sandringham ahead of the christening of the Princess Charlotte on July 5, 2015. Chris Jackson/PA Archive/PA Images

Mike and Zara Tindall with their daughter Mia Tindall at the end of the Artemis Great Kindrochit Quadrathlon on the banks of Loc Tay, Perthshire, Scotland, on July 11, 2015. Andrew Milligan/PA Archive/PA Images

Princess Charlotte is the centre of attention at her christening as the Duke of Edinburgh, Queen Elizabeth II, the Duchess of Cornwall and Prince William stand with the newest member of the royal family as she's held by the Duchess of Cambridge, July 5, 2015. Chris Jackson/PA Archive/PA Images

The 1990s

Press speculation concerning the marriage of the Prince Charles and Princess Diana was rife at the start of the 1990s, but it was Prince Andrew and the Duchess of York who would separate first in March 1992, an event which was swiftly followed in April by the divorce of Princess Anne and Captain Mark Phillips.

During a state visit to Germany in October that year, angry demonstrators in Dresden threw eggs at Her Majesty in protest against the Allied bombing of the city during the Second World War. Then, in November, a large fire broke out at Windsor Castle causing substantial damage. During a speech to mark the 40th anniversary of her accession, Her Majesty famously described 1992 as her "annus horribilis" – Latin for horrible year. Before it was over, Prime Minister John Major had formally announced the separation of the Prince and Princess of Wales.

In the years that followed, both Prince Charles and Princess Diana revealed the intimate details of their marriage breakdown to the press – including the nature of the relationship between the prince and his long-term acquaintance Camilla Parker-Bowles. Due to the ongoing controversies surrounding senior

Queen Elizabeth II and the Duke of Edinburgh inspect the floral tributes laid at the gates of Buckingham Palace on the eve of Princess Diana's funeral September 5, 1997.

members of the royal family and the princess's charity work, she remained a hugely popular figure, even after her divorce from the prince was confirmed in 1996.

A year later, on August 31, 1997, Princess Diana was killed as a result of the injuries sustained during a car crash in Paris. Prince Charles arrived in the French capital the next day to escort his ex-wife's body back to Great Britain.

Queen Elizabeth II was at Balmoral on holiday at the time, and appeared in public shortly after to accompany Princes William and Harry to church along with the Duke of Edinburgh. While the princess had found her way into the hearts of many, few would have predicted the incredible outpouring of public emotion which followed her death and Her Majesty faced criticism for failing to address her nation in the week that followed as she attempted to shield her grandsons from intense press interest.

On Friday, September 5, Queen Elizabeth II broke her silence and spoke to her subjects in a live television address in which she expressed her admiration for Princess Diana and a desire to care for her family as a grandmother.

The public outcry lessened as a result, and attention turned to the funeral which took place the next day at Westminster Abbey. An estimated three million mourners and onlookers flocked to London and it's believed that the worldwide television audience for the ceremony reached two-and-a-half billion as Elton John famously performed a rewritten version of Candle in the Wind and Earl Spencer – brother of the princess – made an emotional speech which drew applause from those in attendance.

The press and public obsession with the affairs of the royal family peaked with the death of Princess Diana. The intense pressure that the media had placed on Queen Elizabeth II, the Duke of Edinburgh and their children subsided as the decade drew to a close. The untimely passing of the princess had had a sobering effect, and the royal family no longer dominated national headlines.

In the aftermath, Queen Elizabeth II steered her family through the difficult times with the sort of dignity that has become her signature. The monarchy accepted that it had to modernise too – and as the 21st century beckoned, a more professional public relations approach was embarked upon in a bid to create a more positive public image of the royal household.

In a speech at a Guildhall luncheon to mark the 40th anniversary of her accession to the throne, Queen Elizabeth II famously brands 1992 her annus horribilis, November 24, 1992.

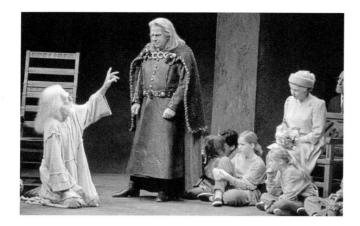

Youngsters from the Children's Shakespeare Festival join Queen Elizabeth II for a performance of King Lear – with Fritz Weaver (left) playing the eponymous character and Jack Ryland as Kent – at the Folger Shakespeare Library in Washington DC, USA, May 16, 1991. Barry Thumma/AP/Press Association Images

During a historic address to a joint session of the US Congress in Washington DC, Queen Elizabeth II is applauded by Vice President Dan Quayle and House Speaker Thomas Foley, May 16, 1991. Doug Mills/AP/Press Association Images

Australian rugby union captain Nick Farr-Jones smiles broadly as he collects the Webb Ellis Cup from Queen Elizabeth II at Twickenham. The Australians beat home side England 12 points to six to win the second Rugby World Cup on November 2, 1991. Adam Butler/PA Archive/PA Images

Dame Vera Lynn talks to Queen Elizabeth II after an event at London's Earls Court to celebrate the 40th anniversary of Her Majesty's accession to the throne, October 26, 1992. Martin Keene/PA Archive/PA Images

President of the Republic of Ireland Mary Robinson stands with Queen Elizabeth II at Buckingham Palace on May 27, 1993. This historic meeting was the first time the countries' two heads of state had met since Irish independence in 1921. Martin Keene/PA Archive/PA Images

Queen Elizabeth II, accompanied by a fireman, inspects the damage at Windsor Castle following a fire which wrecked a large part of the royal house and threatened its rich collection of art and other artefacts on November 21, 1992. Gillian Allen/AP/Press Association Images

On May 6, 1994, the new Channel Tunnel was officially opened linking Great Britain and France by rail. Queen Elizabeth II and the Duke of Edinburgh travelled by Eurostar through the new undersea passage to Calais where they were met by French President François Mitterand for an official opening ceremony. Passenger services commenced in November of that year. Martin Keene /PA Archive/PA Images

Children of Royal Air Force servicemen greet Queen Elizabeth II during a walkabout at RAF Akrotiri on October 23, 1993. Tim Ockenden/PA Archive/PA Images

US President Bill Clinton and his wife Hillary stand with Queen Elizabeth II and the Duke of Edinburgh in the Grand Entrance of Buckingham Palace on November 29, 1995. Mr Clinton was on a three-day state visit to Great Britain and the Republic of Ireland. John Stillwell/PA Archive/PA Images

Paul McCartney talks with Queen Elizabeth II as she leaves the Liverpool Institute for Performing Arts on June 7, 1996. Her Majesty had just opened the centre, which was developed from a concept thought up by the former Beatle six years earlier. Bob Collier/PA Archive/PA Images

South African President Nelson Mandela stands with Queen Elizabeth II on his arrival at Buckingham Palace for a state banquet in his honour, July 9, 1996.

On March 13, 1996, a lone gunmen went on a shooting spree at a school in Dunblane, Scotland, killing 16 children and a teacher. Queen Elizabeth II sent a message of sympathy to the people of Dunblane before making a visit four days later with Princess Anne to lay a wreath at the school gates.

On March 6, 1997, Queen Elizabeth II visited Kingsbury High School in Brent, London, to launch the new royal website. Her Majesty is pictured looking over the shoulder of 17-year-old student Christopher Baily who demonstrates the new site's capabilities. Fiona Hanson/PA Archive/PA Images

Elton John plays a rewritten version of his classic Candle in the Wind during the funeral service of Princess Diana at Westminster Abbey, September 6, 1997. Adam Butler/PA Archive/PA Images

From left to right, the Duke of Edinburgh, Prince William, Earl Spencer, Prince Harry and Prince Charles walk behind the funeral cortege of Princess Diana on September 6, 1997. The Duke of Edinburgh pledged to support his young grandsons who had expressed doubt as to whether they should walk behind their mother as the precesion made its way to Westminster Abbey for the ceremony which was broadcast to an estimated two-and-a-half billion TV viewers. Adam Butler/PA Archive/PA Images

Queen Elizabeth II and the Duke of Edinburgh celebrated their golden wedding anniversary in November 1997 and events were held throughout the year in celebration. Her Majesty is pictured meeting guests, all couples celebrating 50 years of marriage, at a special Buckingham Palace garden party on July 15, 1997. John Stillwell/PA Archive/ PA Images

Prime Minister Tony Blair, Queen Elizabeth II and the Duke of Edinburgh applaud at the opening ceremony of the Millennium Dome in Greenwich which took place on New Year's Eve, 1999. Fiona Hanson/PA Archive/ PA Images

Pop sensations the Spice Girls meet Queen Elizabeth II at the Royal Variety Performance at London's Victoria Palace Theatre on December 12, 1997. From left to right the group are Emma Bunton, Victoria Beckham, Melanie Chisholm, Geri Halliwell (shaking hands with Her Majesty) and Melanie Brown.

French President Jacques Chirac joins Queen Elizabeth II for a joint unveiling of a statue of Sir Winston Churchill in Paris on November 11, 1998. John Stillwell/PA Archive/PA Images

The 2000s

The new millennium brought about a renewed sense of optimism for the royal family who looked to move on from the damaging and tragic events of the 1990s. As preparations were under way for the 2002 Golden Jubilee celebrations, Queen Elizabeth II lost her sister Princess Margaret on February 9, aged 71, and The Queen Mother, on March 30, aged 101.

Royal correspondents and the general media doubted that the jubilee celebrations would be successful given the circumstances. However, an estimated one million people attended each of the three days of celebratory events held in London in a show of support for the monarchy. The enthusiasm on display gave credence to the theory that despite the fractious nature that Queen Elizabeth II had with the media, public support for the sovereign was generally strong and hints of disapproval had often been exaggerated.

Demonstrating her continued devotion to Great Britain and the Commonwealth, Her Majesty and the Duke of Edinburgh travelled more than 40,000 miles during the year taking in trips to the Caribbean, Australia, New Zealand and Canada. While the Golden Jubilee allowed subjects to see their head of state, Queen Elizabeth II herself saw it as a way to thank her peoples for their support.

Further proof that any negative feeling toward the royal family had dissipated came when in 2005 Prince Charles married Camilla Parker-Bowles – who became the Duchess of Cornwall – in a civil ceremony at Windsor Castle, becoming the first member of the British royal family to wed in such a way. Originally scheduled for April 8, the nuptials were delayed one day until April 9 so the prince could attend the funeral of Pope John Paul II.

Internationally, Her Majesty continued to foster healthy relationships and this was evident close to home as the improved situation in both Northern Ireland and the

Republic of Ireland saw Queen Elizabeth II attend the first Maundy service held outside England or Wales in Armagh. In May 2011, Her Majesty and the Duke of Edinburgh made a historic state visit to the Republic of Ireland at the invitation of President Mary McAleese, becoming the first British monarch to enter the country since the 1911 tour by her grandfather King George V when the whole of Ireland was still part of the United Kingdom.

Belying her 80-plus years, Queen Elizabeth II also visited New York in 2010 – giving a speech at the United Nations and opening a memorial garden for the British victims of the September 11 terrorist attacks. Her Majesty and her husband also toured Australia in October 2011, her 16th visit to the Commonwealth Realm.

In 2012, Queen Elizabeth II celebrated 60 years on the throne – and her subjects joined in the party with events held across the United Kingdom and throughout the Commonwealth. In a message released on accession day in February, Her Majesty said: "I hope that this jubilee year will be a time to give thanks for the great advances that have been made since 1952 and to look forward to the future with clear head and warm heart." In this sprit, Queen Elizabeth II and the Duke of Edinburgh travelled the UK extensively while her children and grandchildren made royal visits to Commonwealth members on her behalf.

Later in the same summer, Her Majesty played a central role in another national celebration when she opened the London 2012 Summer Olympic and Paralympic Games, becoming the first head of state to open two Olympics in two different countries – she had also opened the 1976 games in Montreal, Canada. The improved PR effort by Buckingham Palace came into full effect during the opening ceremony when Queen Elizabeth II played herself in a short film alongside Daniel Craig as iconic fictional British secret agent James Bond – a move which was met with huge public support and appreciation.

Santa Claus enlists the help of Queen Elizabeth II to hand out gifts to young racegoers at Ascot, December 16, 2000. Fiona Hanson/PA Archive/PA Images

During a two-day state visit to Slovakia, Queen Elizabeth II makes a speech at the Philharmonic Hall in central Bratislava, October 23, 2008. Chris Ison/PA Archive/ PA Images

Living up to her reputation as 'the People's Queen', Her Majesty shares a joke with well-wishers after two-year-old Lucas Whisker took a tulip from the monarch as she left the Jubilee Library in Brighton, March 8, 2007. Chris Ison/PA Archive/PA Images

Queen Elizabeth II waits to greet guests of a state banquet at the Presidential Palace in Rome, on the first day of a state visit to Italy, October 16, 2000. Fiona Hanson/PA Archive/PA Images

Gold medal winning Team GB members from the 2000 Summer Olympics in Sydney, Australia, meet Queen Elizabeth II at a royal reception on November 16, 2000. Pictured (left to right) are boxer Audley Harrison, rower Steve Redgrave and heptathlete Denise Lewis. Fiona Hanson/PA Archive/PA Images

Continuing her long-standing tradition, Queen Elizabeth II marks Maundy Thursday by distributing Maundy Money to pensioners during a service at Lincoln Cathedral on April 20, 2000. The 148 recipients were all recommended by clergy and ministers of all denominations for services made to their respective communities. John Giles/PA Archive/PA Images

Council for the Protection of Rural England chairman Sir David Ford joins Queen Elizabeth II at a picnic in Windsor Great Park on July 29, 2001, to celebrate the organisation's 75th birthday. Actress Prunella Scales accompanies Sir David and Her Majesty, getting an invitation to the event having recently played Queen Elizabeth II in a TV drama about Soviet spy and art expert Sir Anthony Blunt. John Stillwell/PA Archive/PA Images

On August 4, 2000, The Queen Mother celebrated the momentous occasion of her 100th birthday and was joined on the balcony of Buckingham Palace by daughters Queen Elizabeth II and Princess Margaret to greet the crowd packed into The Mall.

John Stillwell/PA Archive/PA Images

Princess Margaret
1930-2002

Princess Margaret died on February 9, 2002, at the age of 71 having suffered a stroke. Her funeral was held on February 15 and in accordance with her wishes it was a private service for family and friends only. Unlike other royal family members, the princess was cremated and her ashes placed in the tomb of her parents at the King George VI Memorial Chapel at Windsor Castle two months later. A state memorial service was held at Westminster Abbey on April 19, 2002.

Queen Elizabeth The Queen Mother
1900-2002

The Queen Mother died in her sleep aged 101 on March 30, 2002, at Windsor Castle with Queen Elizabeth II at her bedside. A 10-day period of national mourning followed before the funeral took place at Westminster Abbey on April 9. The coffin was laid to rest beside that of her husband King George VI at St George's Chapel in Windsor; seven weeks earlier Princess Margaret had died and her ashes were buried together with those of her mother.

Born Elizabeth Bowes-Lyon, she and her husband had been unexpectedly thrust onto the public stage following the abdication of King Edward VIII. Many royal historians and commentators credit her with making the monarchy more accessible and more accountable to the nation for their behaviour as individuals and as an institution. She invented the now familiar walkabout – a way for royals to meet their subjects face-to-face – and during the wartime Blitz, when many were abandoning London for the country, she insisted that the royal family should remain in the city.

In her role as colonel-in-chief of the Household Cavalry, Queen Elizabeth II, accompanied by the Duke of Edinburgh, arrives at the Presentation of Standards and Guidon ceremony in the Horse Guards Parade on May 21, 2003. Matthew Fearn/PA Archive/PA Images

A naval guard of honour greets Queen Elizabeth II and the Duke of Edinburgh during the royal couple's visit to HMS Victory, June 28, 2005. Anwar Hussein/ EMPICS Entertainment

At a reception for the Women's Royal Voluntary Service at St James's Palace, Queen Elizabeth II meets TV presenter Cilla Black, March 21, 2005. Anwar Hussein/EMPICS Entertainment

US President Barack Obama and First Lady Michelle Obama are welcomed to Buckingham Palace by Her Majesty, April 1, 2009. White House photo

Wearing 3D glasses, Queen Elizabeth II watches a display and pilots a JCB digger during a visit to the University of Sheffield Advanced Manufacturing Research Centre on November 18, 2010. John Giles/PA Archive/PA Images

Veteran entertainer and star of the Royal Variety Bruce Forsyth is knighted by Queen Elizabeth II during an Investiture ceremony at Buckingham Palace on October 12, 2011. Lewis Whyld/PA Archive/PA Images

Queen Elizabeth II plants a tree during a visit to Newmarket Animal Health Trust, October 29, 2009. Chris Jackson/PA Archive/PA Images

At the site of the former World Trade Center, Queen Elizabeth II lays a wreath in remembrance of the victims of the September 11 terrorist attacks in New York, Washington DC and rural Pennsylvania, July 6, 2010. John Stillwel/PA Archive/PA Images

US President Barack Obama and Queen Elizabeth II greet guests at Winfield House, London, ahead of a dinner in honour of Her Majesty held on May 25, 2011. Talking to Queen Elizabeth II is actor Colin Firth, who had won an Oscar the previous year for his portrayal as her father King George VI in The King's Speech. White House photo

At the opening ceremony of the Summer Olympic Games in London on July 28, 2012, Queen Elizabeth II makes a speech and declares the event officially open (above). John Stillwell/PA Archive/PA Images

Her Majesty appeared in a short film playing herself where she joined Daniel Craig's James Bond to 'parachute' into the stadium. Both are pictured (right) in 2006 at the premiere of Craig's first outing as the iconic British spy in Casino Royale. Anwar Hussein/EMPICS Entertainment

The Queen's Award for Enterprise | These awards are among the most prestigious accolades for businesses in the UK. Achievements by British companies are recognised in three categories – international trade, innovation and sustainable development. To be eligible a company must be UK-based with a minimum of two full-time equivalent employees and a track record of outstanding commercial success for more than two years. Winners receive a wide range of benefits including use of the prestigious award emblem on company stationery, websites, goods produced and advertising material. The award is formally conferred by a royal representative, and winners also receive an invitation to a reception hosted by Her Majesty at Buckingham Palace.

The Queen's Award for Enterprise Promotion | This award recognises individuals who make outstanding contributions to enterprise culture in the UK. In contrast to the business awards, individuals are nominated by others who are aware of, and would like to recognise, their enterprising achievements. Individual honours do not expire and recipients are invited, along with those who nominate them, to the Buckingham Palace event.

The winners of both are announced annually on Queen Elizabeth II's birthday, April 21.

Queen Elizabeth II at Buckingham Palace during the reception for the Queen's Awards, 2012. Department for Business, Innovation and Skills/Michael David/BIS Digital *

To mark 100 years since the start of the First World War, the Tower of London hosted the Blood Swept Lands and Seas of Red installation which depicted poppies flowing out of its tallest windows. Queen Elizabeth II is seen inspecting the remembrance tribute on October 16, 2014. Chris Jackson/PA Archive/PA Images

Queen Elizabeth II arrives in a specially charted bus at the Medical Research Council in Cambridge, May 23, 2013. Chris Radburn/PA Archive/PA Images

The Queen's 90th Year

During her 90th year, Queen Elizabeth II became Great Britain's longest-reigning monarch. In her 63 years and counting on the throne much has changed around her but what she does has remained largely unaltered. The monarch has two main roles: official head of state, and symbolic head of the nation.

For the former, Queen Elizabeth II has many official duties including opening Parliament, signing acts of Parliament and holding regular meetings with the prime minister. In May 2015, Her Majesty welcomed David Cameron to Buckingham Palace as he informed the sovereign of his willingness to continue as the leader of the British government following his party's election victory. Although protocol would dictate that Queen Elizabeth II's approval of such matters is a formality, her involvement is a public reminder of the monarchy's function and the responsibilities that she has retained for more than six decades.

Alongside her domestic duties, Her Majesty is an ambassador for Great Britain, receiving foreign dignitaries, entertaining visiting heads of state and making visits overseas in the interests of diplomacy and positive economic relations. Travel has always been important to Queen Elizabeth II – and in 2015, alongside the Duke of Edinburgh, she undertook a four-day tour of Germany during which she delivered a speech at a state dinner in her honour. Acting as head of the nation, Queen Elizabeth II's role is to lead from the front in various social and cultural aspects of British and Commonwealth life. Her Majesty is a role model for national identity, unity and pride and aims to convey the sense of stability that comes with the monarchy, as opposed to the fluid and changing nature of politics. Regular visits to all corners of the United Kingdom allow Queen Elizabeth II to demonstrate these values and characteristics to her subjects, as well as providing the opportunity for people to feel a sense of a personal relationship with the sovereign.

In a wider sense, Her Majesty also reflects the mood of a nation during times of national triumph or tragedy such as sporting success or Remembrance events. The same applies when representing the emotions and thoughts of the country in the aftermath of triumph or tragedy abroad, and this was evident in November 2015 when Queen Elizabeth II sent a message of condolence to President Francois Hollande of France following the terrorist attacks in Paris.

Tying the two strands of the monarchy together is Queen Elizabeth II's ability to recognise achievement; both officially and in terms of the message that such honours send to the nation. Among the thousands of messages sent by Her Majesty each year, famous examples including 100th birthday telegrams – she is able to give personal congratulations to remarkable individuals. Other forms of recognition include the honours lists, awards, patronage and sponsorship. Charitable support is also central to the monarchy, and Queen Elizabeth II enjoys close relationships with – at any given time – around 3000 organisations either as a patron herself or through a member of the royal family.

Schedules may have been reduced and workload may have been managed in recent years, but Queen Elizabeth II continues to execute the duties of the monarchy with vigour as she approaches the milestone of her 90th birthday. Rumours have persisted in recent years that Her Majesty may abdicate the throne and allow Prince Charles to succeed her and in 2014 that speculation came to a head with predictions of an announcement in the annual Christmas broadcast. For many though, the notion that Queen Elizabeth II would give up the monarchy is as unlikely as it is absurd. Nearly 69 years ago, on the occasion of her 21st birthday, Princess Elizabeth took to the airwaves during a trip to South Africa and declared: "My whole life whether it be long or short shall be devoted to your service." Long it most certainly has been, and in those years there has been nothing to suggest that Her Majesty will break her unequivocal vow.

On the way to deliver a speech to open Parliament after the election of a new Conservative government, Queen Elizabeth II travels in a carriage from Buckingham Palace with the Duke of Edinburgh, May 27, 2015. Kirsty Wigglesworth/AP/ Press Association Images

On the day she became Great Britain's longest-reigning monarch, Queen Elizabeth II waves from a carriage window at Edinburgh's Waverley Station after boarding a steam train on which she will travel to inaugurate the new £294 million Scottish Borders Railway, September 9, 2015.
Danny Lawson/PA Wire/Press Association Images

At Yorkshire's Richmond Castle, Queen Elizabeth II attends the amalgamation parade of the Queen's Royal Lancers and 9th/12th Royal Lancers on May 2, 2015. John Giles/PA Archive/PA Images

Arnaud Bamberger accompanies Queen Elizabeth II to present trophies including the Queen's Cup at the Cartier Queen's Cup polo tournament final in Windsor Great Park, June 14, 2015. Jonathan Brady/PA Archive/PA Images

After presenting awards to the first winners of the Queen's Young Leaders Commonwealth project, Her Majesty talks to guests at a Buckingham Palace reception, June 22, 2015. Steve Parsons/ PA Archive/PA Images

German President Joachim Gauck and his partner Daniela Schadt travel by boat along the River Spree in Berlin with Queen Elizabeth II and the Duke of Edinburgh on the first full day of a state visit to Germany, June 24, 2015. Ian Vogler/Daily Mirror/PA Archive/PA Images

Queen Elizabeth II upholds the tradition of the royal walkabout during a state visit to Germany, greeting well-wishers as she departs the Adlon Hotel, June 26, 2015. Chris Jackson/PA Archive/PA Images

Her Majesty smiles as she meets staff during a visit to the Royal Hospital for Sick Children and the Cardiac Rehabilitation Unit Gymnasium on July 3, 2015. She would later unveil three plaques to officially open the Queen Elizabeth University Hospital, the Royal Hospital for Children and the Queen Elizabeth Teaching and Learning Centre in Glasgow. Danny Lawson/PA Archive/PA Images

At Blair Castle, Perthshire, on September 13, 2015, Queen Elizabeth II laughs with Alec Lochore – event director of the Longines Fédération Equestre Internationale European Eventing Championship. Her Majesty presented medals to the winning team. Ian Rutherford/PA Wire/Press Association Images

Pony Major Mark Wilkinson talks to Queen Elizabeth II alongside Royal Regiment of Scotland regimental mascot Cruachan IV on August 10, 2015. Her Majesty had arrived at Balmoral to take up summer residence. Andrew Milligan/PA Wire/Press Association

In the Throne Room at Buckingham Palace, Queen Elizabeth II and the Duke of Edinburgh speak to guests during a reception for the Queen Elizabeth Prize for Engineering, October 26, 2015. Jonathan Brady/PA Wire/Press Association Images

Labour leader Jeremy Corbyn and Prime Minister David Cameron watch as Queen Elizabeth II prepares to lay a wreath during the annual Remembrance Sunday service at the Cenotaph on November 8, 2015. Gareth Fuller/PA Wire/Press Association Images

Patient Verity Thomas, 10, presents Queen Elizabeth II with flowers as head of the NHS trust Tracey Taylor looks on during a tour of the new Birmingham Dental Hospital and School of Dentistry, November 19, 2015. Richard Stonehouse/PA Wire/Press Association Images

Queen Elizabeth II is given a tour of a tram on the Metroline Tramline Extension in Birmingham on November 19, 2015. Chris Radburn/PA Wire/Press Association Images

Maltese president Marie Louise Coleiro Preca talks with Queen Elizabeth II, the Duke of Edinburgh, the Duchess of Cornwall and Prince Charles at an evening reception held in the grounds of San Anton Palace, November 26, 2015. John Stillwell/PA Wire/Press Association Images

At the Mediterranean Conference Centre in Valletta, Malta, Queen Elizabeth II stands in front of the attendees at the opening ceremony for the Commonwealth Heads of Government Meeting on November 27, 2015. Facundo Arrizabalaga/PA Wire/Press Association Images

Away from official engagements, Queen Elizabeth II, Maltese president Marie Louise Colerio Preca and the Duke of Edinburgh are among the crowd watching a polo display at Malta Racing Club, November 28, 2015. Matt Cardy/PA Wire/Press Association Images

At a service of thanksgiving, Queen Elizabeth II meets the congregation before unveiling a plaque at St Columbia's Church in London to celebrate the 60th anniversary of the rededication of the building on December 3, 2015. Jack Hill/The Times/PA Wire/Press Association Images

British actor Martin Clunes is made an OBE by Queen Elizabeth II during an Investiture at Windsor Castle on December 4, 2015. Jonathan Brady/PA Archive/PA Images

Starting the royal family's traditional Christmas break at Sandringham, Queen Elizabeth II and the Duke of Edinburgh arrive at King's Lynn station and will travel to their destination by train, December 17, 2015. Chris Radburn/PA Wire/Press Association Images

In Hillington, Norfolk, Queen Elizabeth II and the Duke of Edinburgh arrive for a morning church service, January 17, 2016. Gareth Fuller/PA Wire/Press Association Images

Queen Elizabeth II leaves the morning Christmas Day service at St Mary Magdalene Church on the Sandringham estate, December 25, 2015. Chris Radburn/PA Wire/Press Association Images

PRESS ASSOCIATION IMAGES,
PAIMAGES.CO.UK

A large majority of the images used in this publication have been sourced from the PA Image collection and archive. Uncredited images are courtesy of PA/PA Archive/PA Images, AP/Press Association Images, PA News/PA Archive/PA Images, PA/ROTA/PA Archive/PA Images, PL/AP/Press Association Images or PA/PA Wire/Press Association Images.

Where applicable, individual credits have been added. The individuals credited are: Adam Butler, Amanda Parks, Andrew Milligan, Andrew Parsons, Anthony Devlin, Anwar Hussein/EMPICS Entertainment, Arrow Press/EMPICS Entertainment, Barratts/S&G Barratts/EMPICS, Barry Batchelor, Barry Thumma, Bethany Clarke, Bob Collier, Cathal McNaughton, Chris Ison, Chris Jackson, Chris Radburn, Christopher Furlong, Danny Lawson, Dave Thompson, David Crump/Daily Mail, David Davies, David Jones, David Parry, Dominic Lipinski, Doug Mills, Duke of York, Eddie Worth, EMPICS Entertainment, Eric Blom, Facudno Arrizabalaga, Fiona Hanson, Gareth Copley, Gareth Fuller, Gillian Allen, Ian Jones/Telegraph pool, Ian Rutherford, Ian Vogler/Daily Mirror, Jack Hill/The Times, Jeff Widener, John Giles, John Stillwell, Jonathan Brady, Kirsty Wigglesworth, Lefteris Pitarakis, Lewis Whyld, Martin Cleaver, Martin Keane, Martin Keene, Martin Rickett, Matt Cardy, Matthew Fearn, Michael Stephens, Oli Scarff, Peter Jordan, Peter Kemp, Richard Stonehouse, Rick Rycroft, Rob Griffith, Ron Bell, S&G/S&G and Barratts/EMPICS Sport, Scott Heppell, Shaun Curry, Sport and General/S&G Barratts/EMPICS, Stefan Rousseau, Steve Parsons, Suzanne Plunkett, Tim Ockenden, Toby Melville and Yui Mok.

CREATIVE COMMONS IMAGES,
CREATIVECOMMONS.ORG

A selection of images used in this publication are published under a Creative Commons Licence. The free, easy-to-use copyright licenses provide a simple, standardised way of giving permission to share the creative work of others on conditions chosen by the work's creator. Images published under a Creative Commons Licence are credited and marked *.

The organisations or individual credited are: Aaron McCracken/Harrisons/Northern Ireland Office, Andy Paradise, paradisephoto.co.uk, Archives New Zealand, Associated Press/Wellcomme Library, London, Australian Photographic Agency/State Library of New South Wales, Brad Saunders, Chatham House, Department for Business, Innovation and Skills/Michael David/BIS Digital, Federal News Photo, Library and Archives Canada, Foreign and Commonwealth Office, Gar Lunney, Library and Archives Canada, Irish123, Jack Hickson/State Library of New South Wales, Library and Archives Canada, Louis St Laurent, Library and Archives Canada, Maurie Wilmott/State Library of New South Wales, MT Hurson/Harrisons/Northern IrelandOffice, National Library of Australia, National Media Museum, New Zealand Defence Force, PolizeiBerlin, Ricardo Stuckert/PR/Agência Brasil, Ryan Higgitt, State Library of New South Wales, State Library of Queensland, State Records NSW, The Co-operative, The National Archives UK and West Midlands Police.

OTHER

A small selection of images taken by American government employees are used in this publication and are published as they exist in the public domain. The organisations or individuals credited are: Gerald R Ford Presidential Library and Museum, John F Kennedy Presidential Library and Museum, NASA, Ronald Reagan Library, United States Library of Congress, US military and the White House.

One image used in this publication is published under the Open Government Licence v3.0. It is credited to Joel Rouse/Ministry of Defence.

All other images used exist in the public domain and/or there are no known copyright restrictions.